The Very BEST of the '90s so far

Project Manager: Carol Cuellar
Cover Design: Odalis Soto

Contents

ALL I WANNA DO

Words and Music by SHERYL CROW, WYN COOPER,
BILL BOTTRELL, DAVID BAERWALD and KEVIN GILBERT

All I Wanna Do - 8 - 1

noon on Tues-day in a bar__ that fac - es a gi - ant car wash. And the

good peo - ple of the world are wash - ing their cars on their lunch break,

hos - ing and scrub-bing as best__ they can_____ in skirts and suits.__

Bridge:

They drive___ their shin - y Dat - suns and Bu - icks

back to the phone *com-pan-y, the re-cord store too._*   Well, they're_ noth-ing like

% *Chorus:*

Bil-ly and me._ 'Cause all I wan-na   do   is have some fun,____   I got a feel-

-ing I'm not the on - ly one. All I wan-na do   is have some fun,_

— I got a feel - ing I'm not the on - ly one. All I wan-na

8

un - til the sun comes up o - ver San - ta Mon - i - ca Boul - e - vard._

Verse 3:
I like a good beer buzz early in the morning,
And Billy likes to peel the labels from his bottles of Bud
And shred them on the bar.
Then he lights every match in an oversized pack,
Letting each one burn down to his thick fingers
Before blowing and cursing them out.
And he's watching the Buds as they spin on the floor.
A happy couple enters the bar dancing dangerously close to one another.
The bartender looks up from his want ads.
(To Chorus:)

ALWAYS BE MY BABY

Words and Music by
MANUEL SEAL, JERMAINE DUPRI
and MARIAH CAREY

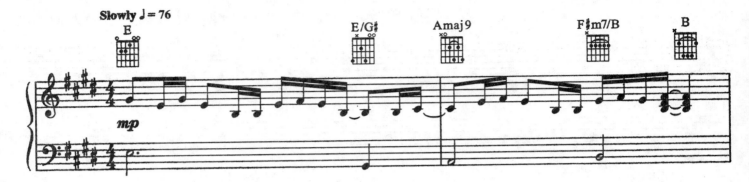

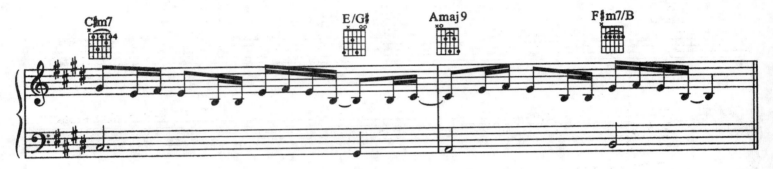

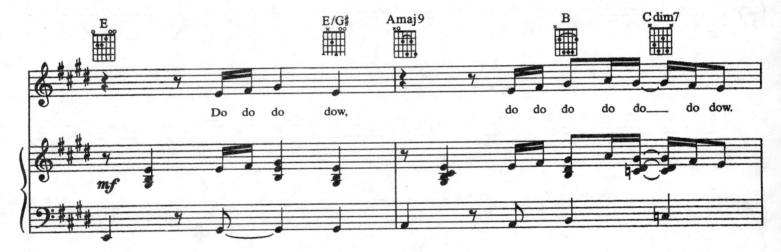

Do do do dow,   do do do do do___ do dow.

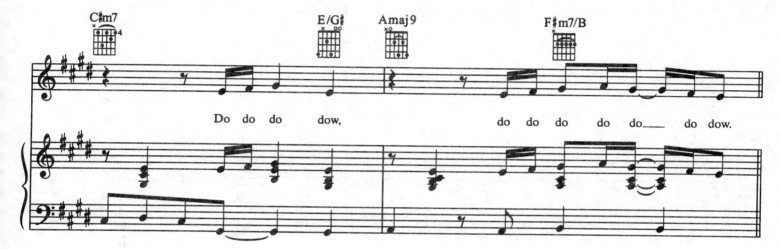

Do do do dow,   do do do do do___ do dow.

Verse:

1. We were as one,___ babe,_____ for a mo-ment in___ time.___
2. I ain't gon-na cry,___ no,_____ and I won't beg you to___ stay.___

And it seemed ev-er-last-ing,_____ that you would al-ways be mine.___
If you're de-ter-mined to leave,_ boy,_____ I will not stand in your way._____

14

Now you want to be free,_____ so I'll let you fly._____
But in-ev-i-ta-bly,_____ you'll be back a - gain._____

'Cause I know in my heart, babe,_____ our_____ love_____ will nev-er die, no.
'Cause you know in your heart, babe,_____ our_____ love_____ will nev-er end, no.

Chorus:

You'll al-ways be a part of me,_____ I'm part of you in-def-i-nite-ly._____

Boy, don't you know you can't es - cape__ me, ooh, dar - ling, 'cause you'll al - ways be__ my ba -

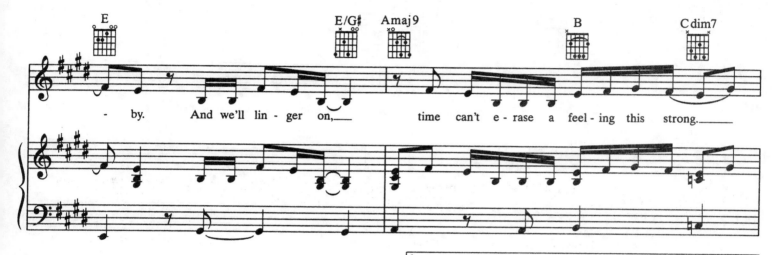

- by. And we'll lin - ger on,___ time can't e - rase a feel - ing this strong.___

1.

No__ way you're ev - er gon - na shake__ me,___ oh, dar - ling, 'cause you'll al - ways be__ my ba -

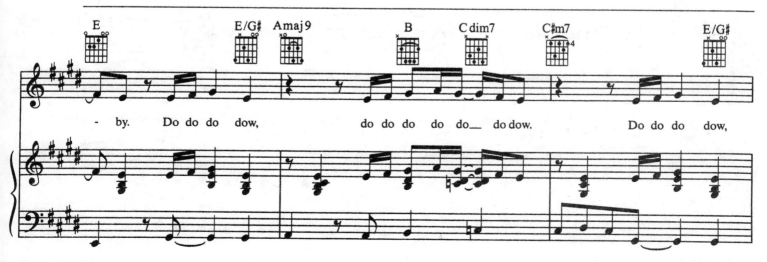

- by. Do do do dow, do do do do do__ do dow. Do do do dow,

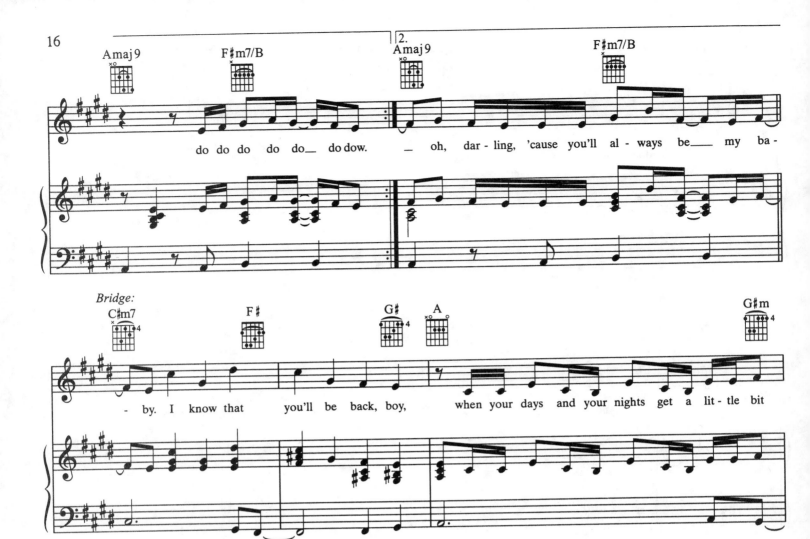

do do do do do do dow. __ oh, dar - ling, 'cause you'll al - ways be__ my ba -

Bridge:

- by. I know that you'll be back, boy, when your days and your nights get a lit - tle bit

cold - er. I know that__ you'll be right back. Oh,

ba - by, be - lieve me, it's on - ly a mat - ter of time,__ time.__

Chorus:

You'll al-ways be a part of me,___ I'm part of you in-def-i-nite-ly.___

Boy, don't you know you can't es-cape___ me, ooh, dar-ling, 'cause you'll al-ways be___ my ba-

-by. And we'll lin-ger on,___ time can't e-rase a feel-ing this strong.___

No___ way you're ev-er gon-na shake___ me,___ oh, dar-ling, 'cause you'll al-ways be___ my ba-

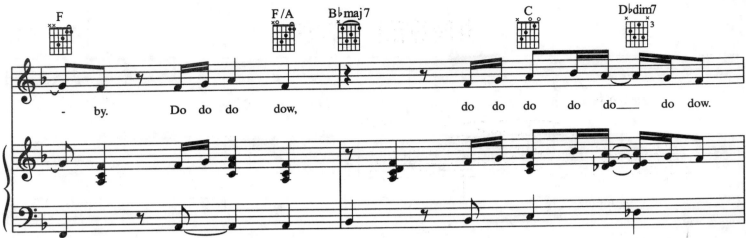

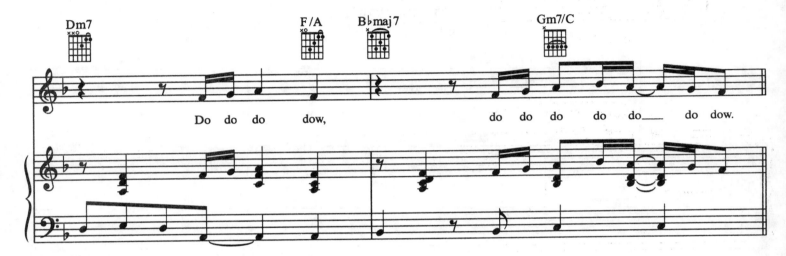

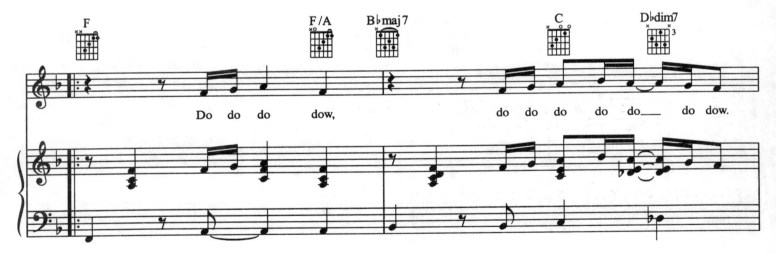

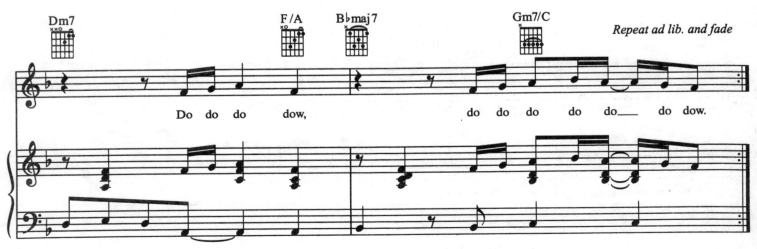

ANGEL EYES

Composed by
JIM BRICKMAN

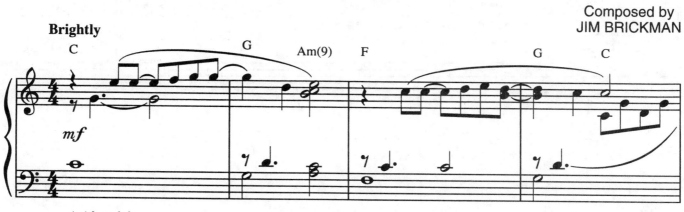

(with pedal)

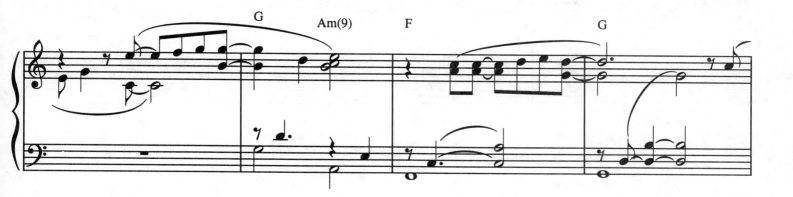

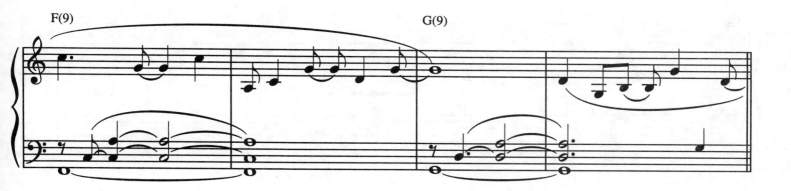

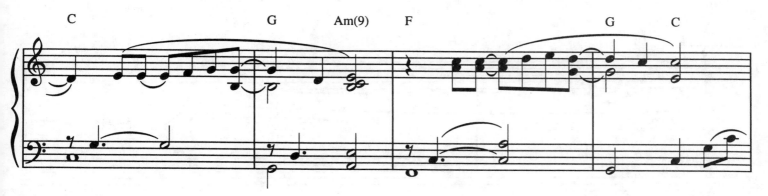

Angel Eyes - 5 - 1

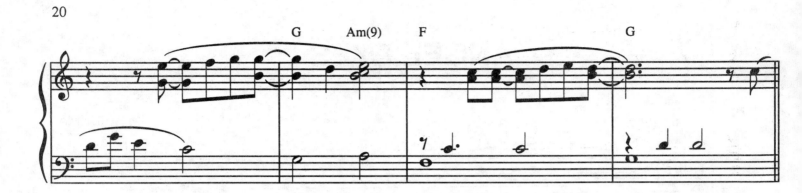

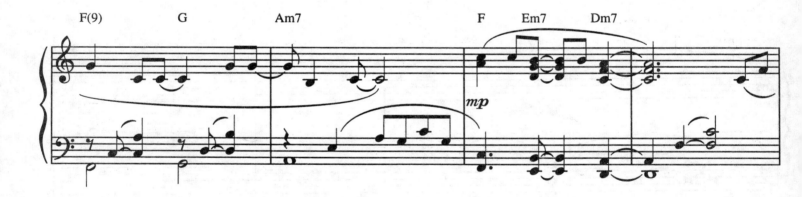

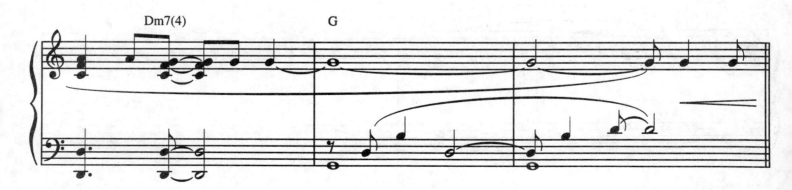

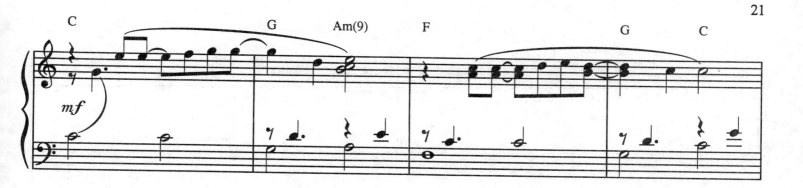

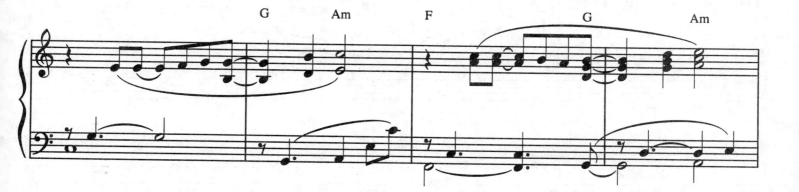

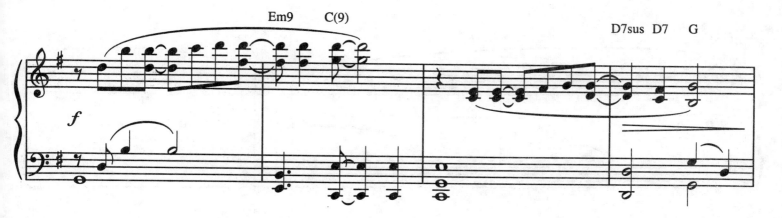

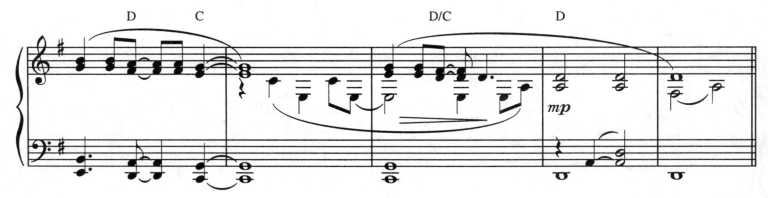

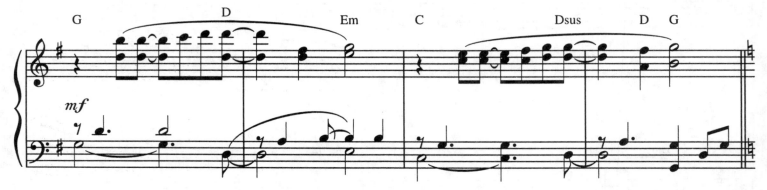

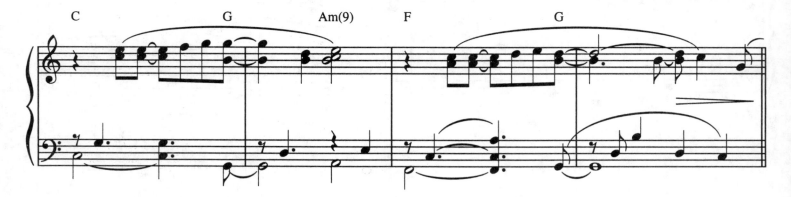

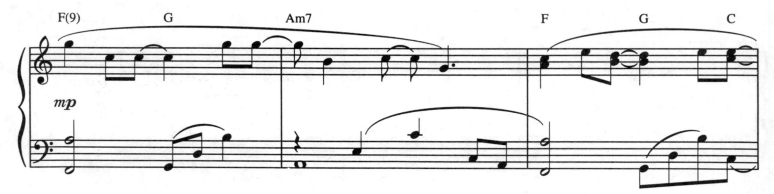

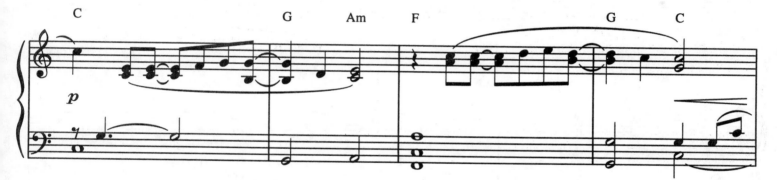

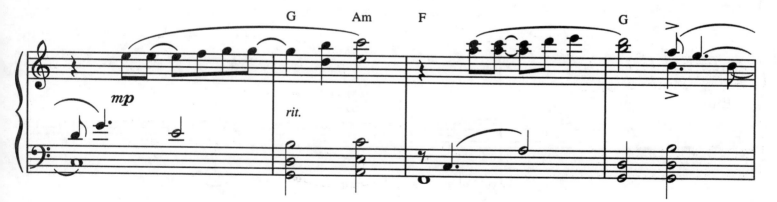

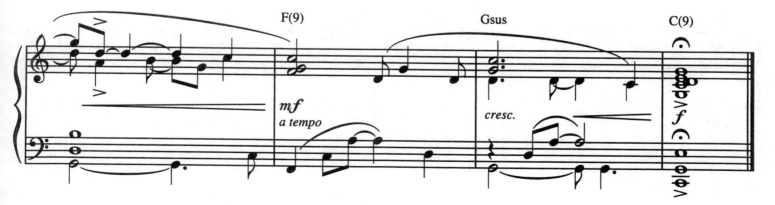

AS LONG AS YOU LOVE ME

By
MAX MARTIN

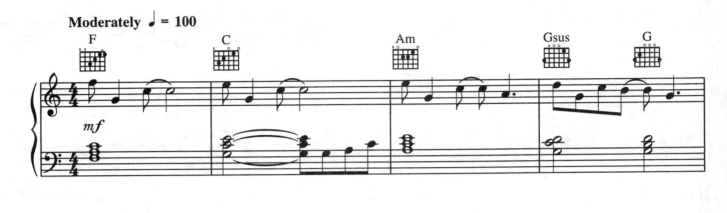

1. Al-though

Verse 1:

lone - li - ness has al - ways been a friend of ___ mine, ___ I'm

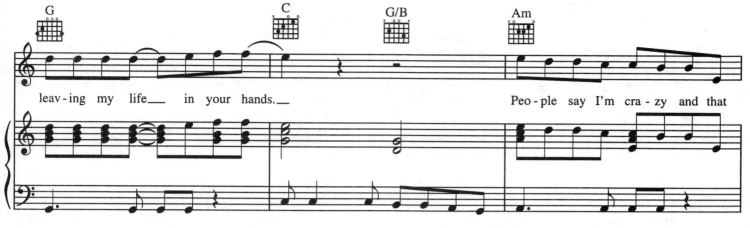

leav-ing my life___ in your hands.___ Peo-ple say I'm cra-zy and that

I am___ blind_____ risk-ing it all___ in a glance._____

Verses 2 & 3:

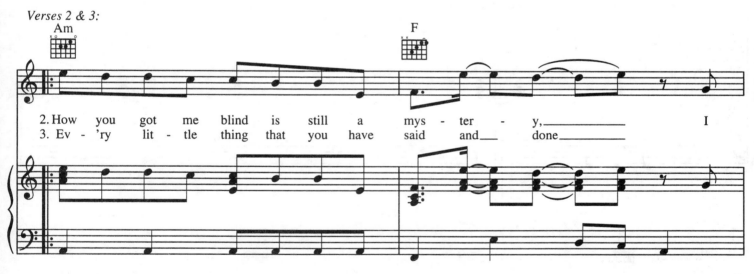

2. How you got me blind is still a mys-ter-y,_____ I
3. Ev-'ry lit-tle thing that you have said and done_____

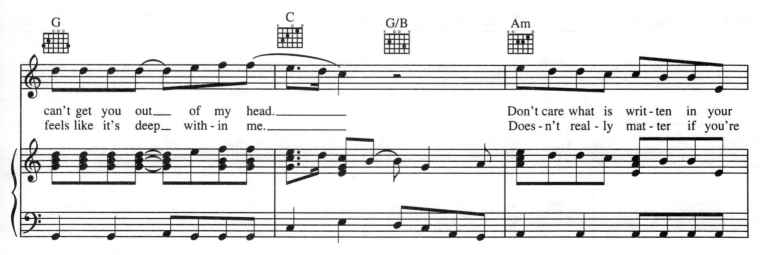

can't get you out___ of my head._____ Don't care what is writ-ten in your
feels like it's deep___ with-in me._____ Does-n't real-ly mat-ter if you're

his-to-ry_ _____ as long as you're here_ with me._
on the_ run,_ _____ it seems like we're meant_ to be._

I don't care who_

Chorus:

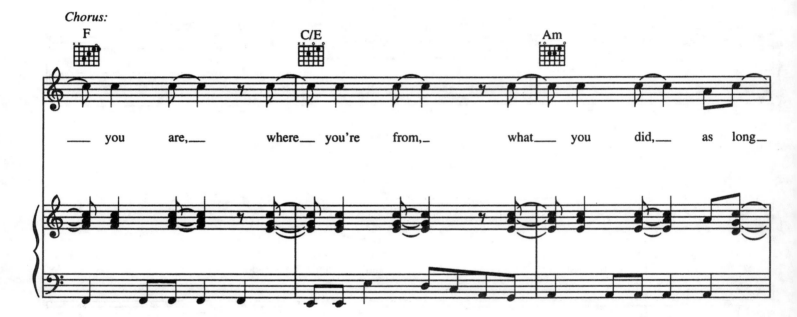

_ you are,_ where_ you're from,_ what_ you did,_ as long_

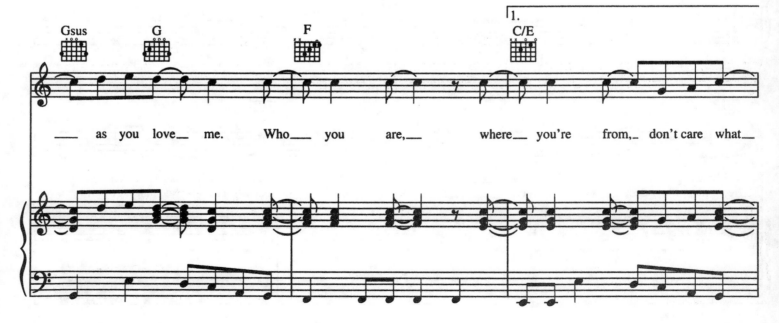

_ as you love_ me. Who_ you are,_ where_ you're from,_ don't care what_

28

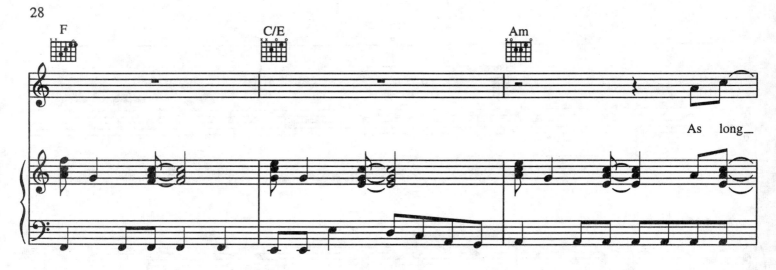

As long_

_ as you love_ me._____ I've tried to hide it so that no one knows, but I guess

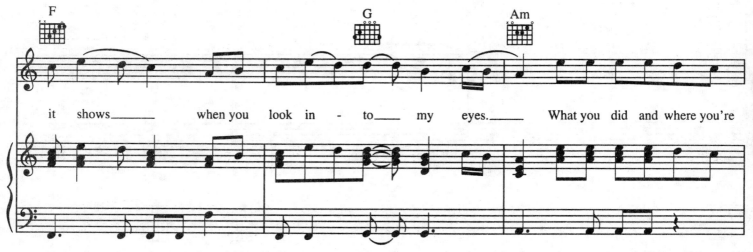

it shows_____ when you look in - to_ my eyes._____ What you did and where you're

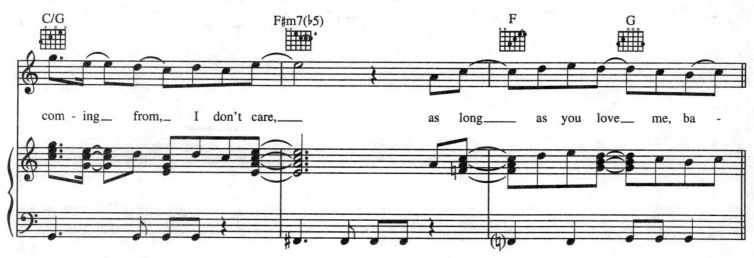

com - ing_ from,_ I don't care,___ as long_____ as you love_ me, ba -

As Long As You Love Me - 7 - 5

From the Twentieth Century Fox Motion Picture
"ANASTASIA"

AT THE BEGINNING

Lyrics by LYNN AHRENS

Music by STEPHEN FLAHERTY

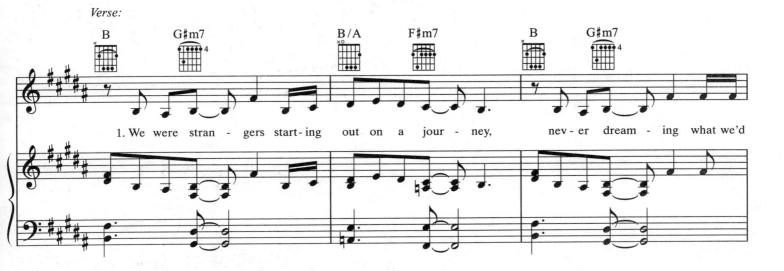

At the Beginning - 7 - 1

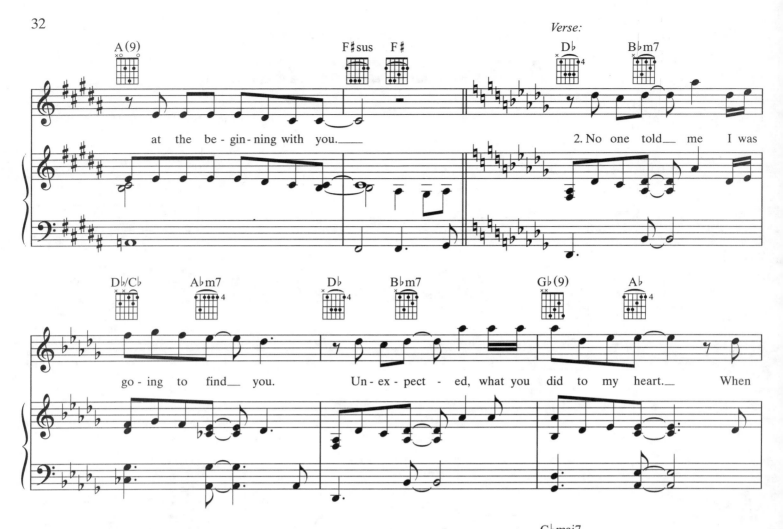

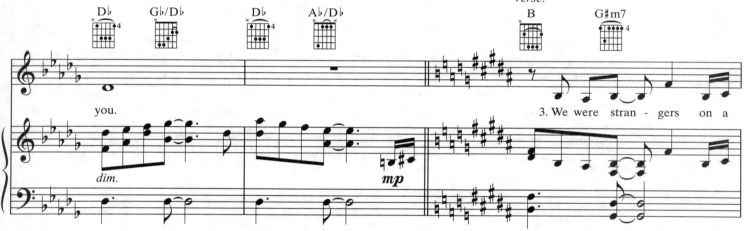

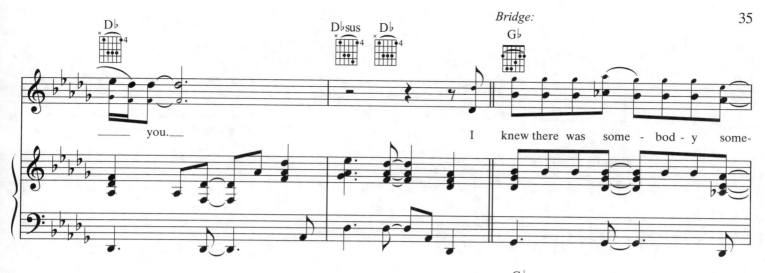

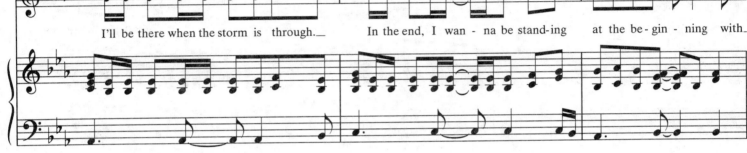

on._____ Start-ing out on a jour-ney. Life is a road, and I want to keep go-ing.

Love is a riv-er, I wan-na keep flow-ing. In the end, I wan-na be stand-ing at the be-gin - ning_____

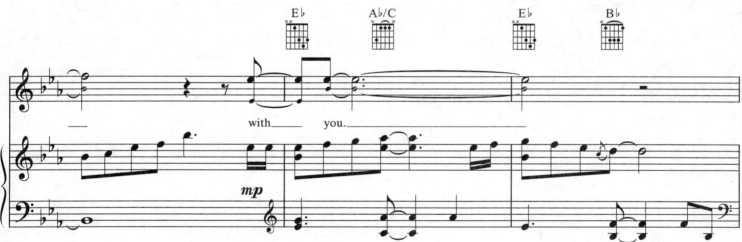

with_____ you._____

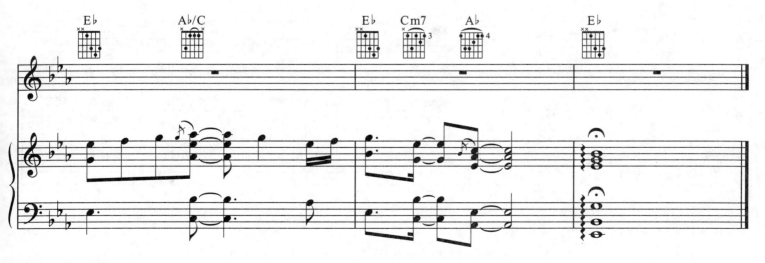

BECAUSE YOU LOVED ME
(Theme from "Up Close & Personal")

Words and Music by
DIANE WARREN

1. For all those times you stood by me, for all the
wings and made me fly, you touched my

truth that you made me see, for all the joy you brought to my life, for all the
hand, I could touch the sky. I lost my faith you gave it back to me. You said no

wrong that you made right, for ev - ery dream you made come true, for all the
star was out of reach, you stood by me and I stood tall. I had your

Because You Loved Me - 5 - 1

light in the dark,___ shin - ing your love___ in - to my___ life.___ You've

been my in - spi - ra - tion,_____ through the lies,___ you were___ the truth. My

D.S. % al Coda

world is a bet - ter place be - cause___ of you.___ You were___ my

loved___ me. You were___ my strength when I___ was weak, you were___ my

BREAKFAST AT TIFFANY'S

Words and Music by
TODD PIPES

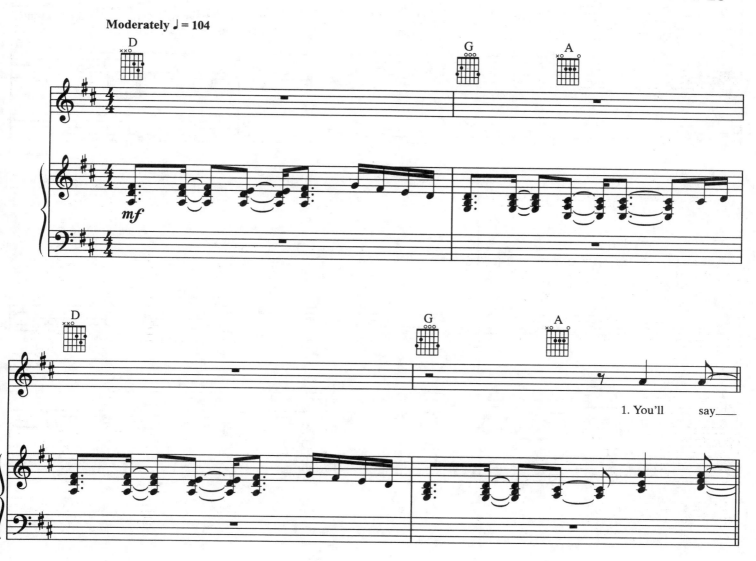

Moderately ♩ = 104

1. You'll say___

Verse:

___ see you,___ the we got noth - ing in com - mon, no but
3. You'll say___ we got noth - ing in com - mon, no

Breakfast at Tiffany's - 5 - 1

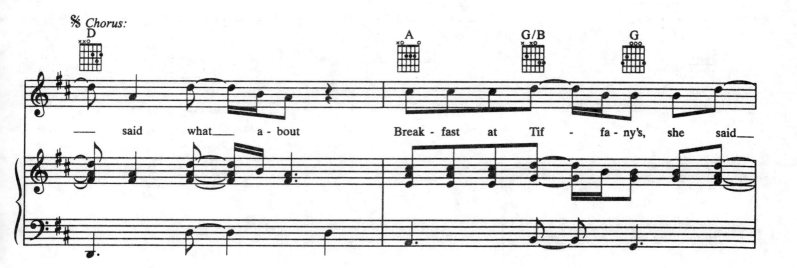

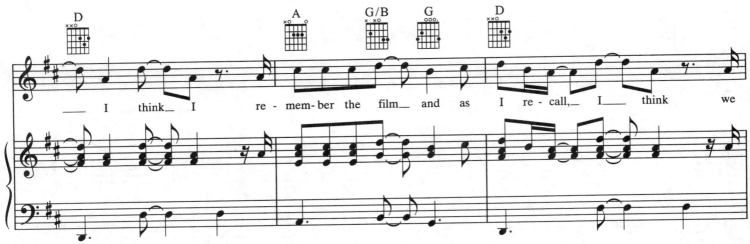

I think__ I re-mem-ber the film__ and as I re-call,__ I__ think we

both kind of liked__ it, and I said well,__ that's the one thing we got.__

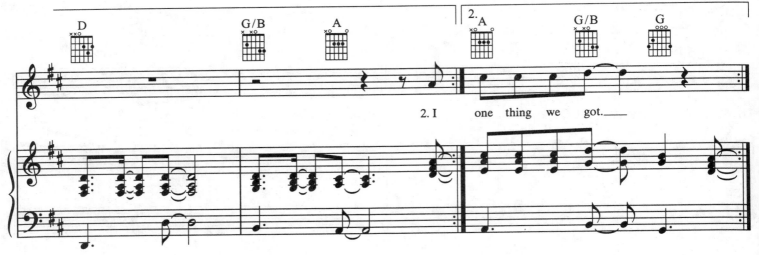

2. I one thing we got.__

BUTTERFLY KISSES

Words and Music by
BOB CARLISLE and RANDY THOMAS

hug ev-'ry morn-ing and but-ter-fly kiss-es at night.___

Verse 2:

2. Sweet six-teen___ to-day;___ she's look-ing like_ her ma-ma a lit-tle

more ev-'ry day.___ One part wom-an, the oth-er part girl;___ to

per-fume and make-up from rib-bons and___ curls;___ try-ing her wings_ out in a

CAN'T STOP THIS THING WE STARTED

Lyrics and Music by
BRYAN ADAMS and
R.J. LANGE

Can't Stop This Thing We Started - 5 - 1

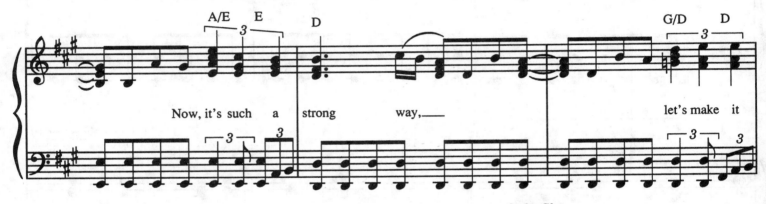

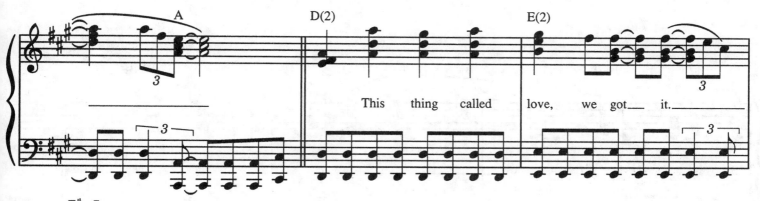

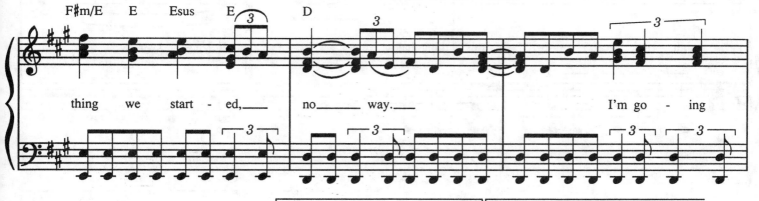

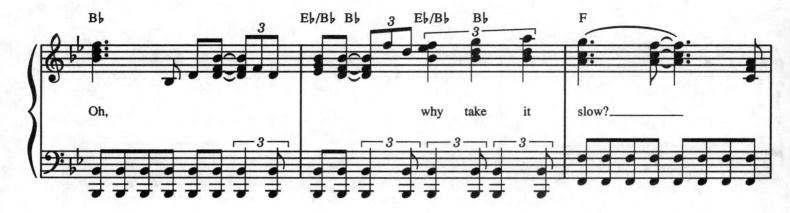

Oh,   why take it slow?_____

I got-ta know,_____   hey, 'cause

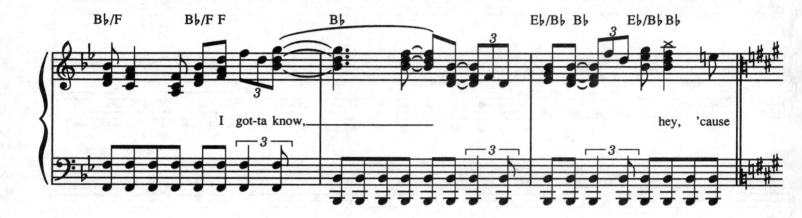

noth - ing can stop this thing that we've got.   (Instrumental solo . . .

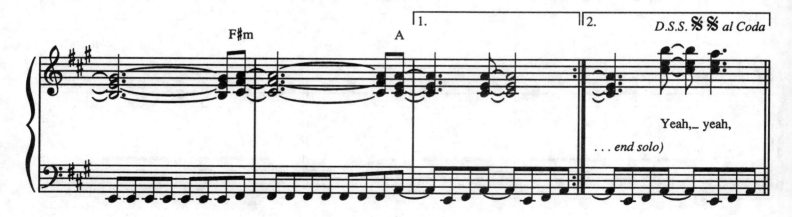

Yeah,_ yeah,

. . . end solo)

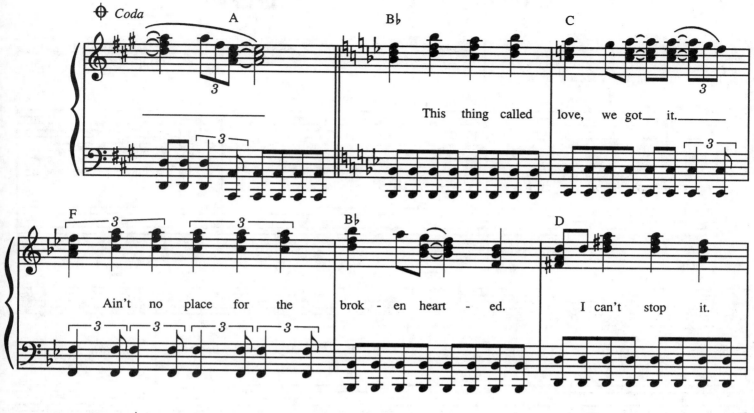

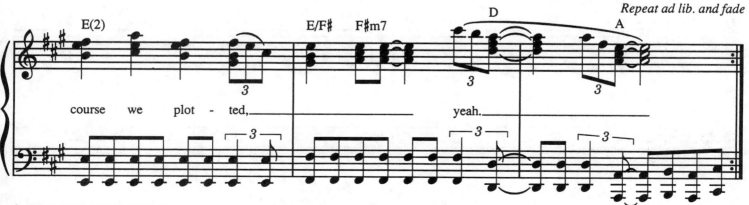

Can't Stop This Thing We Started - 5 - 5

COME TO MY WINDOW

Words and Music by
MELISSA ETHERIDGE

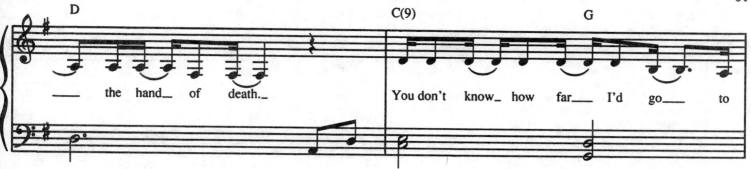

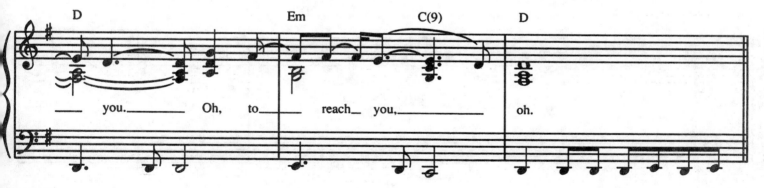

Chorus:

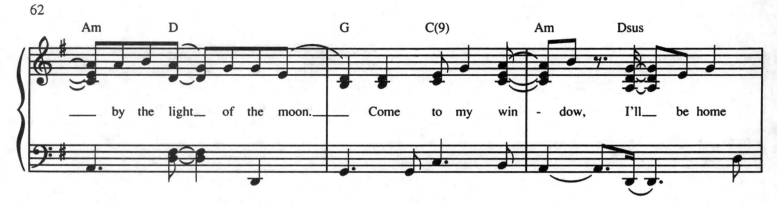

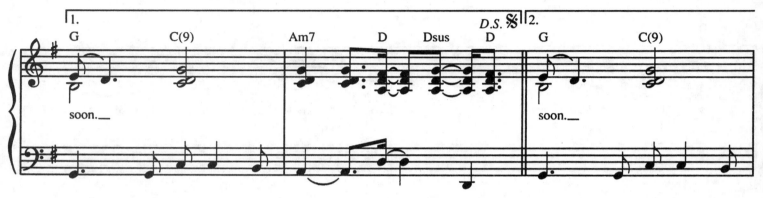

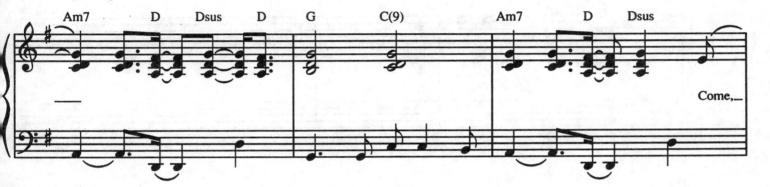

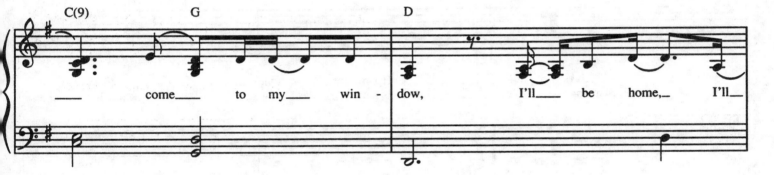

Verse 2:
Keeping my eyes open, I cannot afford to sleep.
Giving away promises I know that I can't keep.
Nothing fills the blackness that has seeped into my chest.
I need you in my blood, I am forsaking all the rest.
Just to reach you,
Just to reach you.
Oh, to reach you.
(To Chorus:)

COMING OUT OF THE DARK

Words and Music by
GLORIA ESTEFAN, EMILIO ESTEFAN, JR.
and JON SECADA

Gospel rock ♩ = 66

1. Why be a-fraid_____ if I'm not a-lone?_____ Life is nev-er
2. Start-ing a-gain_____ is part of_ the_ plan,_____ and I'll be so much

eas - y,_____ the rest is__ un - known.____ And up till now for
strong - er_____ hold-ing__ your_ hand.____ Step by step I'll

Coming Out of the Dark - 5 - 1

FALLING INTO YOU

Words and Music by
MARIE CLAIRE D'UBALDO,
BILLY STEINBERG and RICK NOWELS

Falling Into You - 5 - 1

COUNT ON ME

Words and Music by
BABYFACE, WHITNEY HOUSTON
and MICHAEL HOUSTON

Count on Me - 6 - 1

CUTS BOTH WAYS

Words and Music by
GLORIA ESTEFAN

Slowly ♩ = 88

1. It cuts both ways.__

Our love is like a knife__ that cuts both ways.__ It's driv - en deep__ in - to my

Cuts Both Ways - 4 - 1

Emaj⁷   C#m^{7(♭5)}/G   B²

heart each time___ that I re - a - lize___ how it cuts both ways.___

G#m⁷

Can't be to - geth - er, can - not live a - part.___ We're head - ing straight in - to a

Emaj⁷   C#m^{7(♭5)}/G

bro - ken___ heart,___ but I can't___ stop.___ 'Cause I feel

Slower and soulfully ♩ = 72
Chorus:
Emaj⁷

___ too much___ to let you go.___ I'm hurt - ing you,___ and it's hard___ I know___ to stay

D#m⁷   G#m⁷

___ and fight___ for what we've got,___ know - ing it - 'll nev - er be good e - nough.___ 'Cause you

Emaj⁷

_and I___ are dan-ger-ous.___ We want too much,___ and life ain't___ that way.___ Don't ask_

D♯m⁷

_for more,___ don't be a fool.___

1.
C♯m⁷   C♯m⁷(♭5)/G

Have-n't we al-read-y bro-ken ev-ery rule?___

D.S. 𝄋

Slowly ♩ = 88

2.
C♯m⁷   C♯m⁷(♭5)/G

_dim.
mp

2. It Have-n't we al-read-y bro-ken ev-ery rule?___

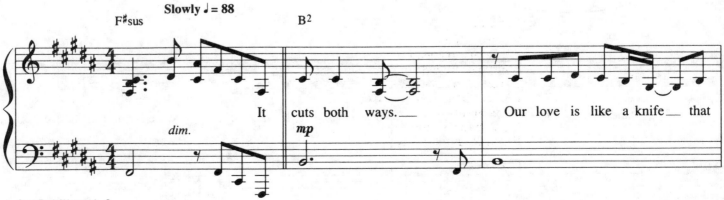

Slowly ♩ = 88

F♯sus   B²

_dim.   mp

It cuts both ways.___ Our love is like a knife___ that

G#m7

Emaj7

cuts both ways.__ It's driv-en deep__ in-to my heart each time__ I see we're

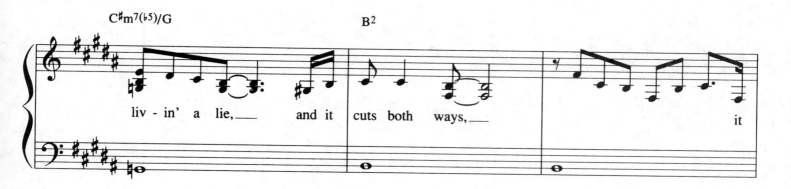

C#m7(b5)/G

B2

liv-in' a lie,__ and it cuts both ways,__ it

G#m7

Emaj7

cuts both ways.__ Mm,_____ it cuts both ways,__

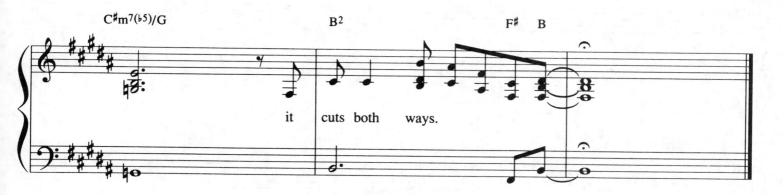

C#m7(b5)/G

B2

F#   B

it cuts both ways.

Verse 2:

It cuts both ways.
We're in too deep for sorry alibis.
Can't have regrets or even question why
We can't say goodbye,
Because it cuts both ways.
No more illusions of the love we make.
No sacrifice would ever be too great
If you would just stay.

(To Chorus:)

DON'T CRY

Words and Music by
SEAL

Don't be so hard on your-self, those tears are

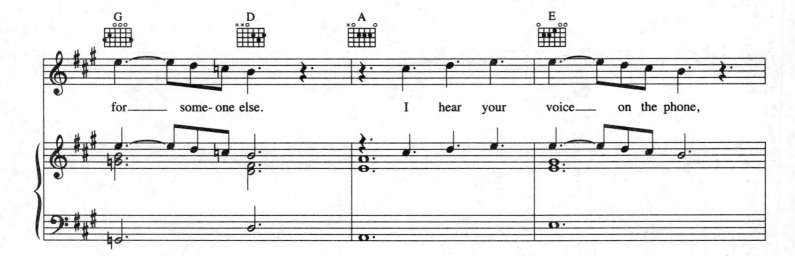

for some-one else. I hear your voice on the phone,

I hear you feel so a-lone, my ba-by,

Don't Cry - 6 - 1

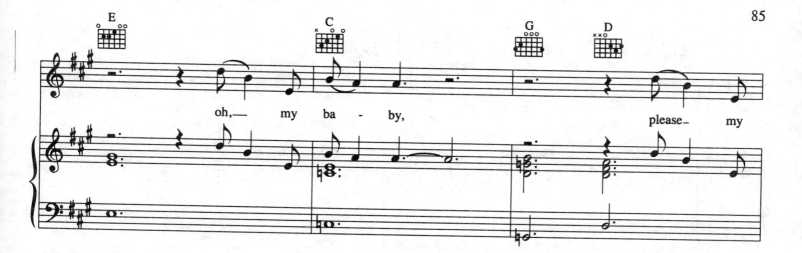

oh,— my ba - by, please— my

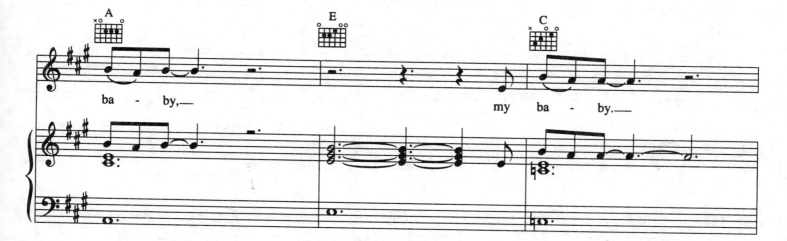

ba - by,— my ba - by.—

a tempo

1. When

Don't Cry - 6 - 2

we were young— and truth was pa-ra-mount———— we were
(Verses 2 & 3 see block lyric)

old-er then and we lived a life with-out—— a-ny doubt,— those

me-mor-ies,— they seem so long a-go,———— what's be-

come of them,— when you feel like me I want— you to know.— Don't

done to me——— is now the warmth in my bed,————————— in my

D.%. al Coda

head,——————— in my head,——————— in my— head. 3. The

Coda

—— to-night sweet ba - by,— don't cry,—————————— don't

cry,————————— 'cause you'll

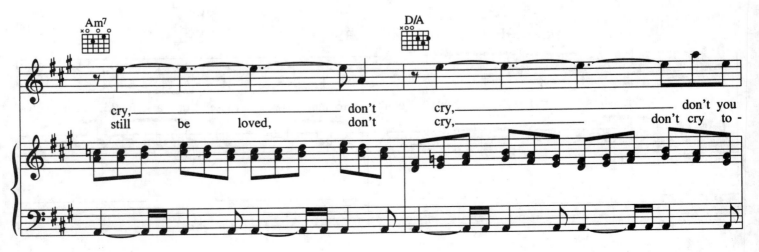

cry,——————— don't cry,————————— don't you

still be loved, don't cry, don't cry to -

Verse 2:
Today I dream
Of friends I had before,
And I wonder why
The ones who care don't call anymore.
My feelings hurt,
But you know I overcome the pain,
And I'm stronger now,
There can't be a fire unless there's a flame.

Don't cry, you're not alone,
Don't cry tonight my baby.
Don't cry, you'll always be loved,
Don't cry.

Verse 3:
The challenges we took
Were hard enough,
They get harder now,
Even when we think that we've had enough.
Don't feel alone
'Cause it's I you understand.
I'm your sedative,
Take a piece of me whenever you can.

Don't cry, you're not alone, (Don't be so hard on yourself)
Don't cry tonight my baby. (Those tears are for someone else)
Don't cry, you'll always be loved, (I hear your voice on the phone)
Don't cry, tonight sweet baby. (I hear you feel so alone)

DREAMING OF YOU

Words and Music by
TOM SNOW and
FRANNE GOLDE

Moderately ♩ = 88

Verse:

1. Late at night when all the world___ is sleep-ing, I stay up and think of you.___ And I
wish on a star___ that some-where you are___ think-ing of me, too.___ 'Cause I'm

Chorus:

dream - ing ___ of you to - night. Till to - mor - row, ___ I'll be

hold-ing you tight. ___ And there's no - where in ___ the world I'd rath - er be than

here in my room, ___ dream-ing a - bout ___ you and me. _____

2. Won-der if you ev - er see_____ me and I won-der if you know I'm there._____
3. I just wan-na hold you close_____ but so far, all I have are dreams of you._____

If you looked in my eyes,_____ would you see what's in - side?__ Would you
So, I wait for the day_____ and the cour - age to say__ how much

e - ven care?_____
I love you._____

Yes, I do. I'll be

FOOLISH GAMES

Words and Music by
JEWEL KILCHER

Moderately slow ♩ = 66

(with pedal)

Verse:

1. You took____ your____ coat off____ and stood in the
2.3.4. *See additional lyrics*

rain,____ you're al-ways cra - zy like_ that.____

And I watched_ from my____ win - dow, al-ways felt I was

* *Vocal sung one octave lower*

Foolish Games - 3 - 1

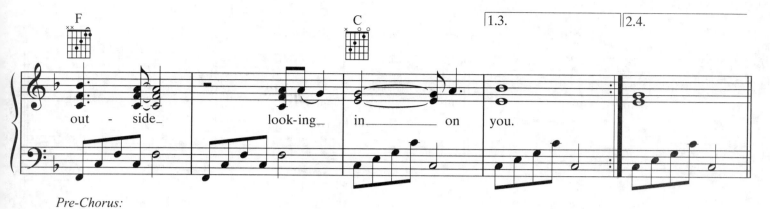

1.3. | 2.4.

out - side_ look-ing_ in_____ on you.

Pre-Chorus:

1. In case_ you failed to no-tice, in case you failed to see,
2. *See additional lyrics*

this is_ my heart_ bleed - ing_ be-fore you, this is me down_ on_ my_ knees.

Chorus:

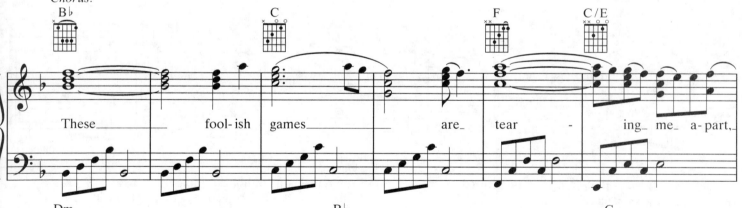

These_____ fool-ish games_____ are_ tear - ing_ me a-part,

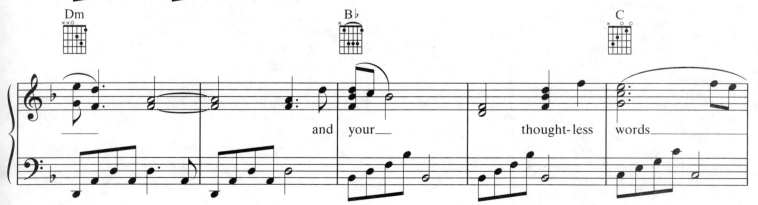

and your___ thought-less words___

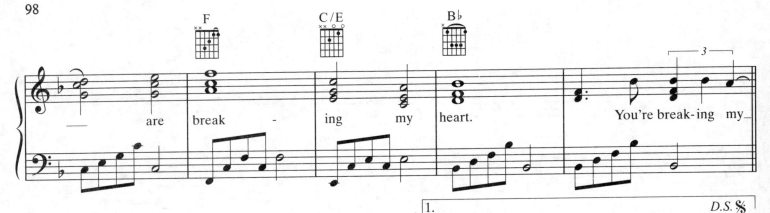

Verse 2:
You're always the mysterious one with
Dark eyes and careless hair,
You were fashionably sensitive
But too cool to care.
You stood in my doorway with nothing to say
Besides some comment on the weather.
(To Pre-Chorus:)

Verse 3:
You're always brilliant in the morning,
Smoking your cigarettes and talking over coffee.
Your philosophies on art, Baroque moved you.
You loved Mozart and you'd speak of your loved ones
As I clumsily strummed my guitar.

Verse 4:
You'd teach me of honest things,
Things that were daring, things that were clean.
Things that knew what an honest dollar did mean.
I hid my soiled hands behind my back.
Somewhere along the line, I must have gone
Off track with you.

Pre-Chorus 2:
Excuse me, think I've mistaken you for somebody else,
Somebody who gave a damn, somebody more like myself.
(To Chorus:)

FOR YOU I WILL

Words and Music by
DIANE WARREN

Chorus:

o - cean for you,__ I will go and bring you the moon,__ I will be your he - ro, your strength,__ an - y - thing__

__ you need. I will be the sun in your sky,__ I will light your way for all time,__ prom - ise you,__

__ for you,__ I will.__ Prom - ise you,__ for you, I will.__

Freely

I prom - ise you,__ for you, I will.__

rit.

From the Twentieth Century-Fox Motion Picture "ONE FINE DAY"

FOR THE FIRST TIME

Words and Music by
JAMES NEWTON HOWARD,
ALLAN RICH and JUD FRIEDMAN

Slowly ♩ = 62

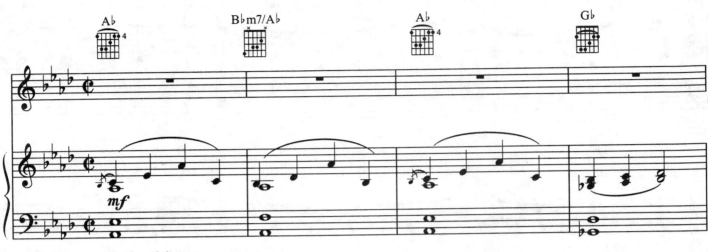

(with pedal)

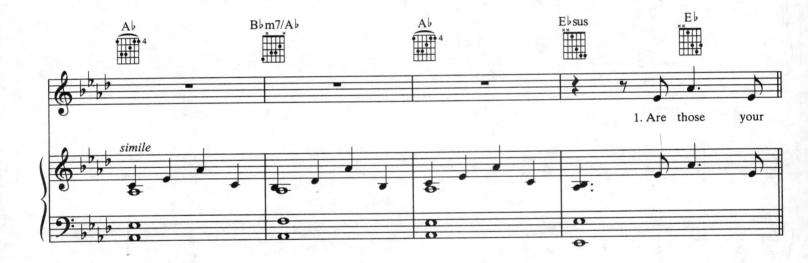

simile

1. Are those your

Verse:

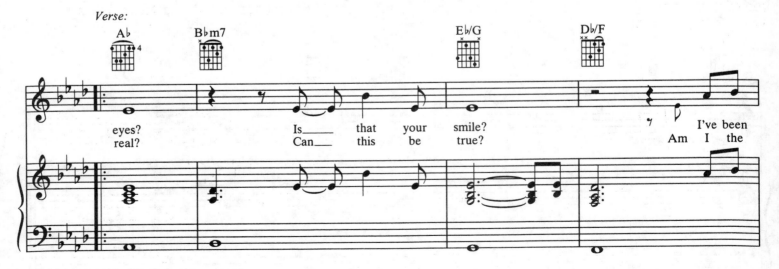

eyes?
real?

Is___ that your smile?
Can___ this be true?

I've been
Am I the

For the First Time - 6 - 1

Now I un-der-stand___ what_____ love___ is,

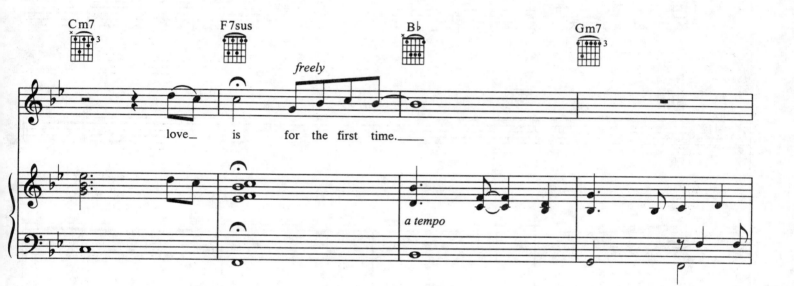

love___ is for the first time.___

freely

a tempo

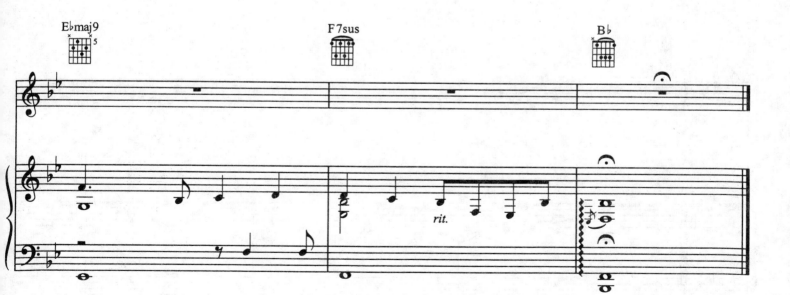

rit.

(I Wanna Take) FOREVER TONIGHT

Words and Music by
ANDY GOLDMARK and ERIC CARMEN

Chorus:

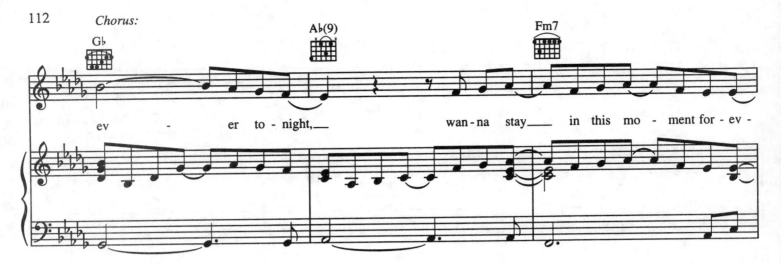

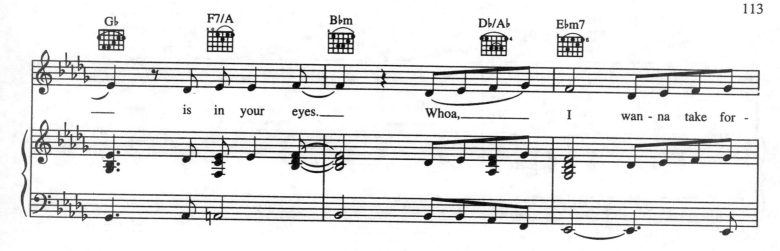

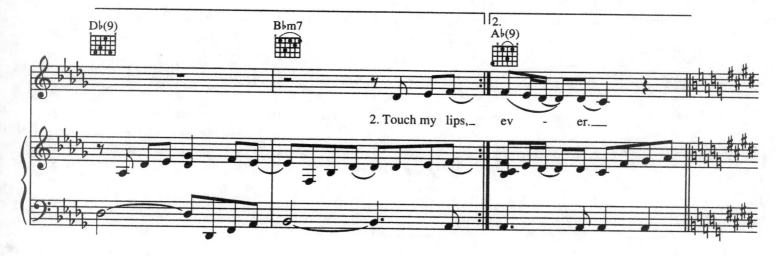

114

Chorus:

(I Wanna Take) Forever Tonight - 6 - 5

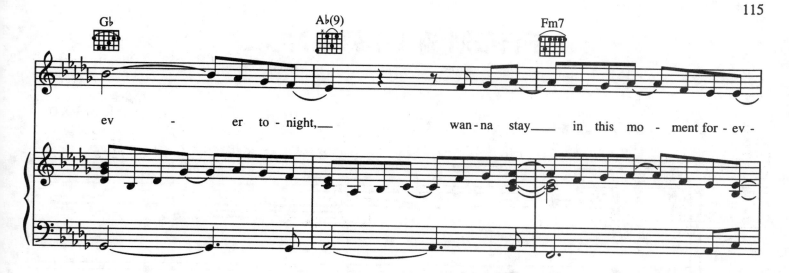

ev - - er to - night,___ wan - na stay___ in this mo - ment for - ev -

- er. I'm gon - na give you all the love that I've got.___ 'Cause I can't live with - out___

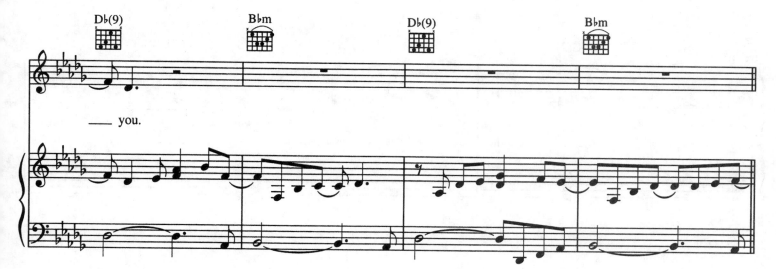

___ you.

Repeat ad lib. and fade

FROM A DISTANCE

Lyrics and Music by
JULIE GOLD

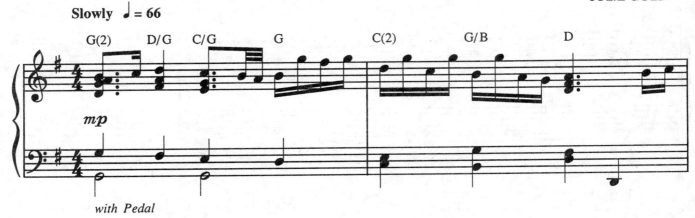

From a Distance - 4 - 1

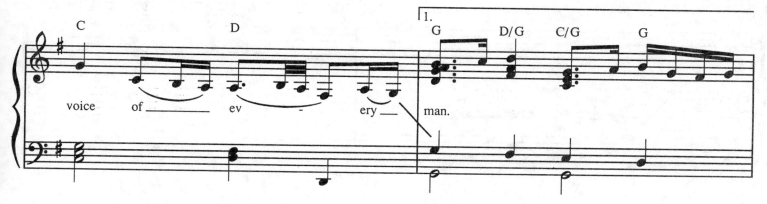

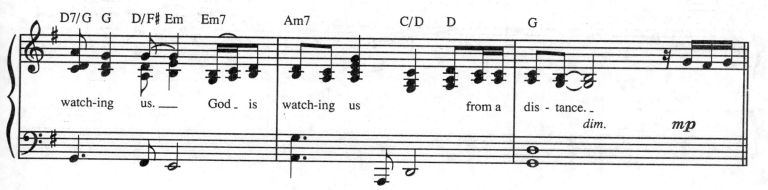

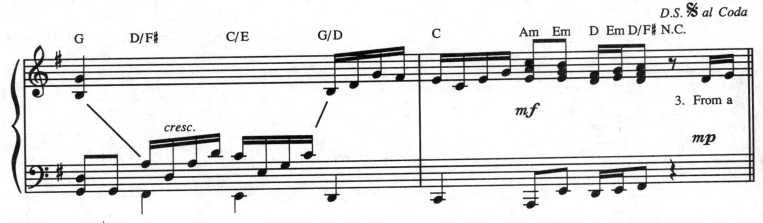

D.S. %️ al Coda

man. _____ And God _ is | watch-ing us. _ God _ is | watch-ing us _ God _ is

cresc.   *f*

watch-ing us | from a _ dis - tance. _____ Oh, God is _ | watch-ing us _____ from a

rit.   *dim.*   *mp slower*

dis - tance.

Verse 2:
From a distance, we all have enough,
And no one is in need.
There are no guns, no bombs, no diseases,
No hungry mouths to feed.
From a distance, we are instruments
Marching in a common band;
Playing songs of hope, playing songs of peace,
They're the songs of every man.
(To Bridge:)

Verse 3:
From a distance, you look like my friend
Even though we are at war.
From a distance I just cannot comprehend
What all this fighting is for.
From a distance there is harmony
And it echos through the land.
It's the hope of hopes, it's the love of loves.
It's the heart of every man.

GOTHAM CITY

Words and Music by
R. KELLY

1. Look-ing o-ver the sky-line of____ the cit-y.____
2. Sleep-ing a-wake be-cause____ of fear.____

Gotham City - 5 - 1

I BELIEVE I CAN FLY

Words and Music by
R. KELLY

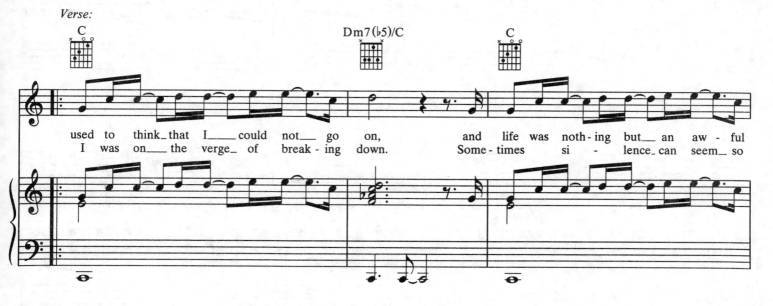

used to think__ that I____ could not__ go on, and life was noth-ing but__ an aw-ful
I was on__ the verge__ of break-ing down. Some-times si - lence__ can seem__ so

I Believe I Can Fly - 5 - 1

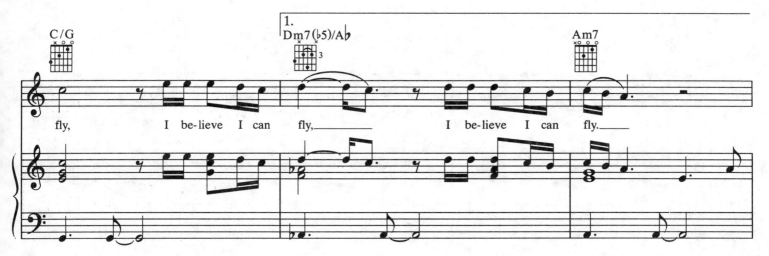

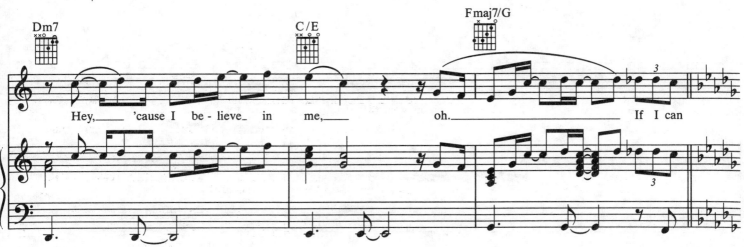

I Believe I Can Fly - 5 - 3

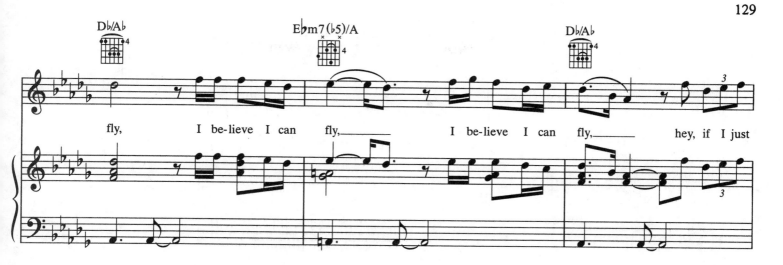

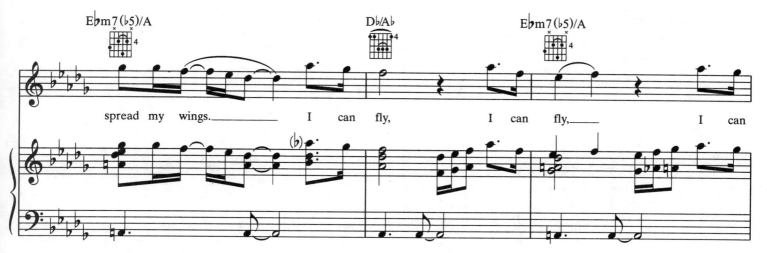

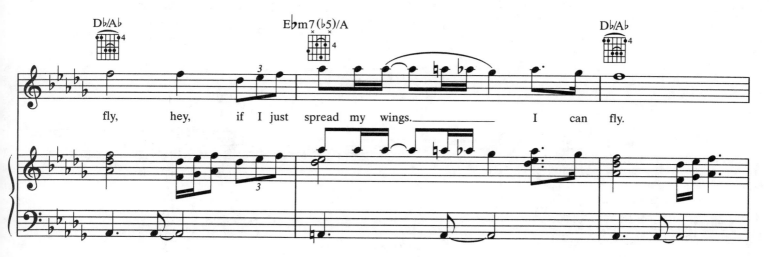

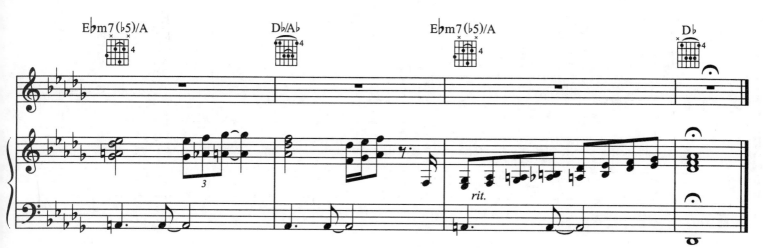

I Believe I Can Fly - 5 - 5

From the Touchstone Motion Picture "CON AIR"

HOW DO I LIVE

Words and Music by
DIANE WARREN

Moderately slow ♩ = 92

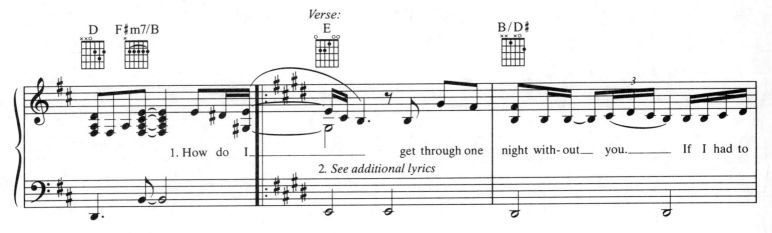

1. How do I get through one night with-out you. If I had to

2. *See additional lyrics*

live with-out you, what kind of life would that be? Oh, I, I need you in my

arms, need you to hold. You're my world, my heart, my soul. If you ev-er leave,

How Do I Live - 4 - 1

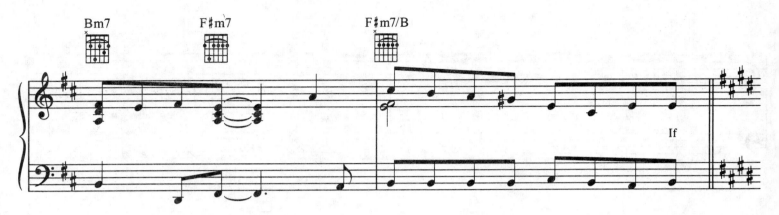

If

you ev-er leave,_____ ba-by, you would take a-way___ ev-'ry-thing.___

Need you with me._____ Ba-by, 'coz you know that you're ev – 'ry-thing___

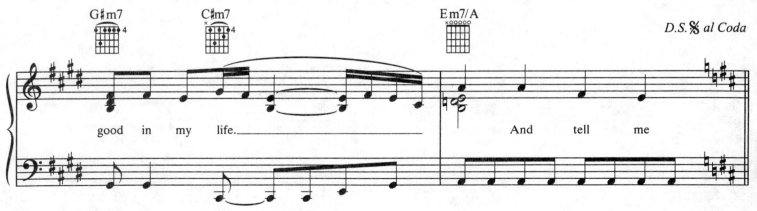

D.S. 𝄋 *al Coda*

good in my life._____ And tell me

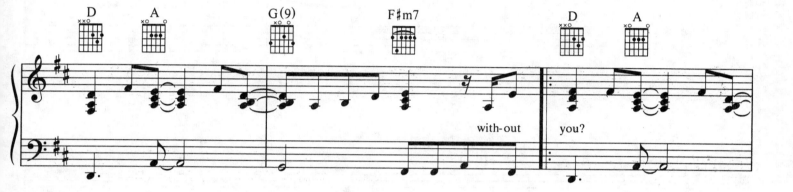

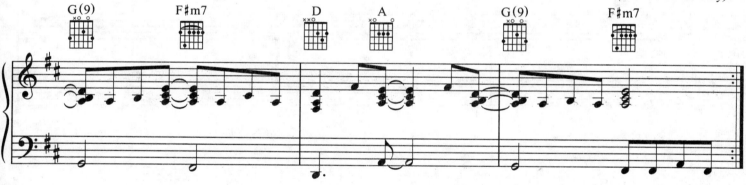

Verse 2:
Without you, there'd be no sun in my sky,
There would be no love in my life,
There'd be no world left for me.
And I, baby, I don't know what I would do,
I'd be lost if I lost you.
If you ever leave,
Baby, you would take away everything real in my life.
And tell me now...
(To Chorus:)

From the Motion Picture "THE PREACHER'S WIFE"

I BELIEVE IN YOU AND ME

Words and Music by
SANDY LINZER and DAVID WOLFERT

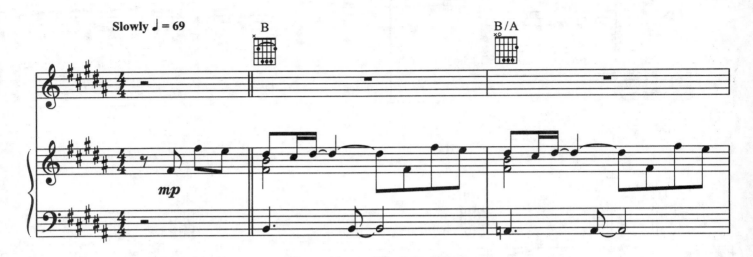

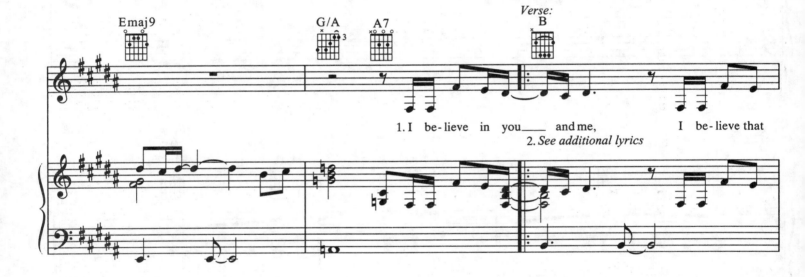

1. I be-lieve in you___ and me, I be-lieve that
2. *See additional lyrics*

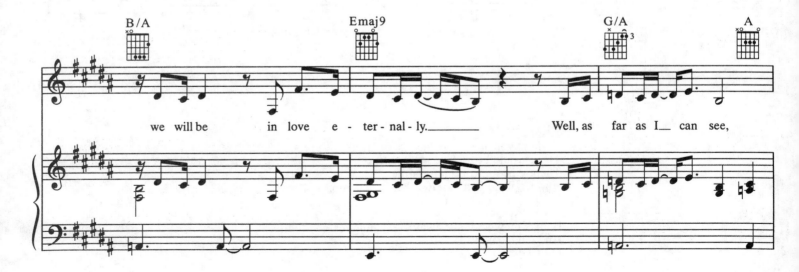

we will be in love e-ter-nal-ly.___ Well, as far as I can see,

I Believe in You and Me - 4 - 1

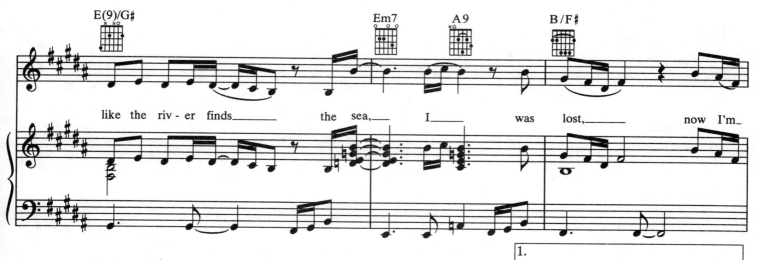

Verse 2:

I will never leave your side,
I will never hurt your pride.
When all the chips are down,
I will always be around,
Just to be right where you are, my love.
Oh, I love you, boy.
I will never leave you out,
I will always let you in
To places no one has ever been.
Deep inside, can't you see?
I believe in you and me.
(To Bridge:)

I CAN LOVE YOU LIKE THAT

Words and Music by
STEVE DIAMOND, MARIBETH DERRY
and JENNIFER KIMBALL

Verse:

read you Cin-der-el-la, you hoped it would come true;__ that one day your Prince Charm-ing would come
nev-er make a prom-ise I don't in-tend to keep,__ so when I say for-ev-er, for-

res-cue you._____ You like ro-man-tic mov-ies, and you nev-er will for-get the
ev-er's what I mean. I'm no Ca-sa-no-va, but I swear this much is true:

way you felt when Ro-me-o kissed Ju-li-et._____ And all this time that you've been__ wait-
I'll be hold-ing noth-ing back when it comes to you.____ You dream of love that's ev-er-last-

-ing. You don't have to wait no__ more._____ I can love you like that,__
-ing, ba-by, op-en up your__ eyes._____

(EVERYTHING I DO) I DO IT FOR YOU

Lyrics and Music by
BRYAN ADAMS, R.J. LANGE
and M. KAMEN

(Everything I Do) I Do It for You - 5 - 1

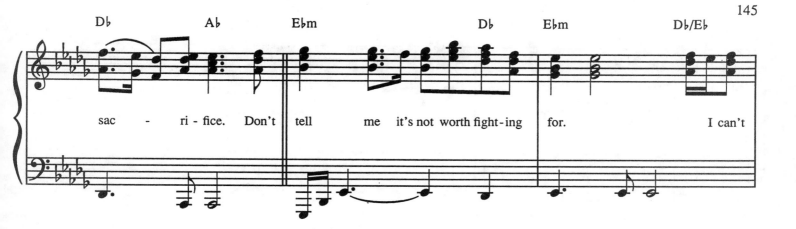

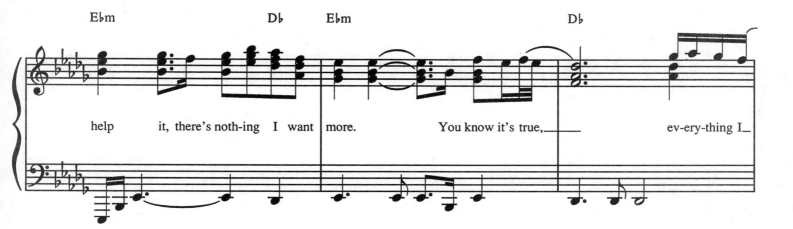

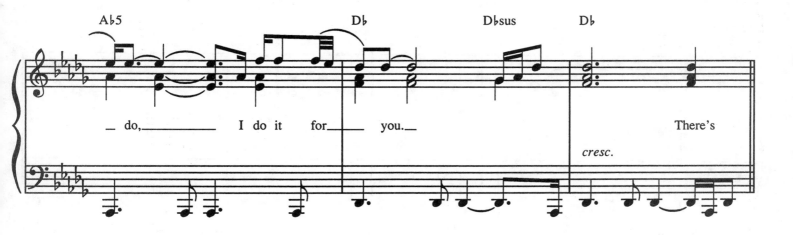

more___love. There's no - where___ un - less you're__ there, all the

time,_____ all the way,___ yeah.___

dim.　　　*mf*

(instrumental solo . . .

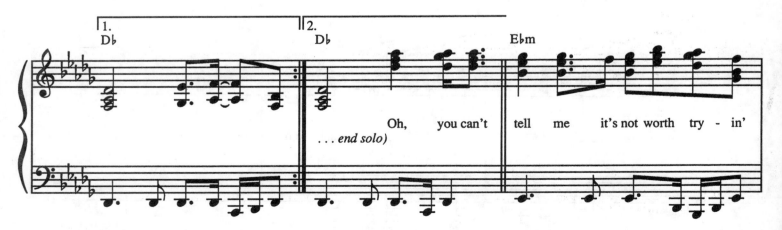

1.　　　　　　　　　　2.

Oh, you can't tell me it's not worth try - in'

. . . end solo)

for.___ I can't help___ it, there's noth-ing I want more. Yeah,___ I would

fight_ for you,___ I'd lie___ for you,___ walk the wire___ for you,___ yeah,___ I'd

die for___ you.___ You know it's true, ev-ery-thing I___

___ do,___ oh,___ I do it for___ you.

(Everything I Do) I Do It for You - 5 - 5

From the Motion Picture "THE MIRROR HAS TWO FACES"

I FINALLY FOUND SOMEONE

Words and Music by
BARBRA STREISAND, MARVIN HAMLISCH,
R.J. LANGE and BRYAN ADAMS

I Finally Found Someone - 8 - 1

151

I Finally Found Someone - 8 - 4

I LOVE YOU ALWAYS FOREVER

Words and Music by
DONNA LEWIS

Moderately ♩ = 102
Verse:

1. Feels like__ I'm stand-ing__ in a time-less__ dream of light mists__ of pale am - ber rose. Feels like__ I'm lost in a deep cloud__ of heav - en - ly scent,__ touch - ing,__ dis - cov - er - ing you.

"I Love You Always Forever" is inspired by the H.E. Bates novel *"Love for Lydia."*
Chorus/Bridge lyric courtesy of *Michael Joseph Ltd.* and *The Estate of H.E. Bates.*

Verse 3:
You've got the most unbelievable blue eyes I've ever seen.
You've got me almost melting away as we lay there
Under blue sky with pure white stars,
Exotic sweetness, a magical time.
(To Chorus:)

I SEE YOUR SMILE

Words and Music by
JON SECADA and
MIGUEL A. MOREJON

Moderately slow ♩ = 80

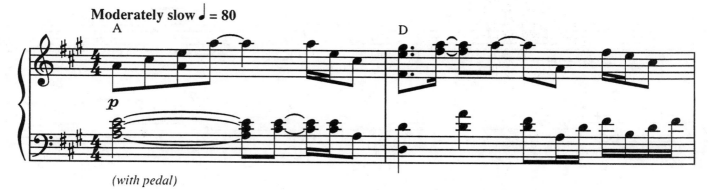

(with pedal)

Verse:

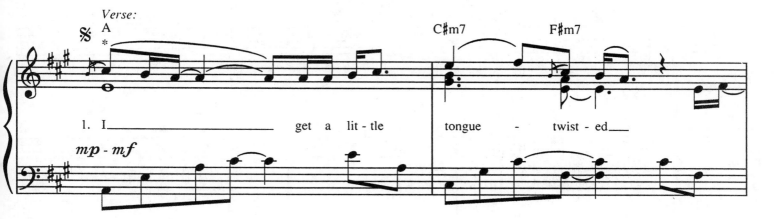

1. I_____ get a lit-tle   tongue - twist-ed___

ev-'ry time I talk_ to you_ when I   see_ you._____ And

Melody is sung one octave lower.

I See Your Smile - 5 - 1

I'm_____ so glad that you just missed it,_____

the way I stared to mem-o-rize_ your face, to kiss_ you in_ my mind,_

_ love_____ you all_____ the time._____ *cresc.*

Chorus 1 & 2:

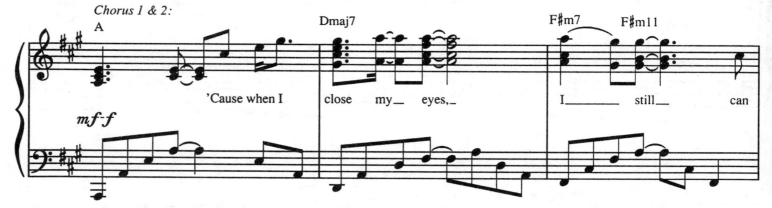

'Cause when I close my_ eyes,_ I_____ still_ can

see your smile._____ It's bright e-nough_ to light my_ life_

out_____ of_____ my dark - est_ hour._____ Please_ be-lieve_ it's true_

— when I tell_____ you, "I_____ love_ you."

_____ you, "I_____ love_ you."_____ Woah,_____ oh.

cresc.

_ƒ_

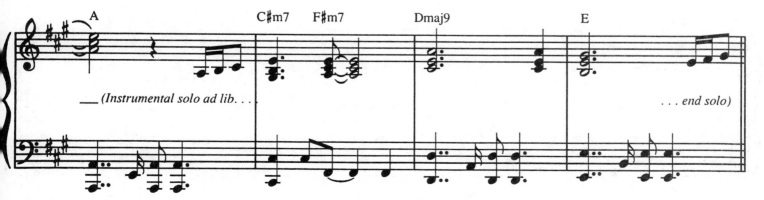

_ (Instrumental solo ad lib. . . . . . end solo)

out____ of____ my dark - est__ hour.___ dark - est__ hour.___

dim.

mp I know_ now this is true___ when I tell____ you, "I____ love_ you."_

_ *dim.* *p*

Ooh,_____ oh yeah._____ *freely* *10*

rit.

Verse 2:
I've taken too many chances,
Searching for the truth in love that's in my heart.
Tell me if I've made the wrong advances;
Tell me if I've made you feel ashamed.
'Cause I know I have to do this;
Would you hold my hand right through it?
(To Chorus:)

From "MY BEST FRIEND'S WEDDING"

I SAY A LITTLE PRAYER

Words by
HAL DAVID

Music by
BURT BACHARACH

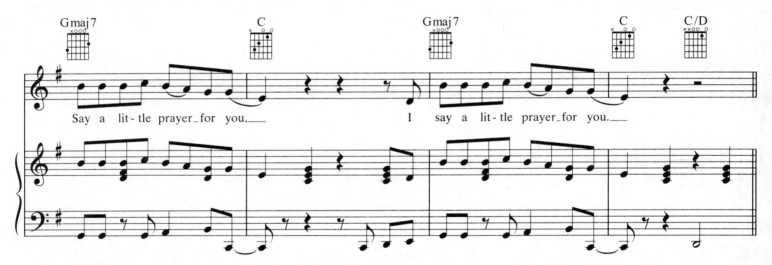

I Say a Little Prayer - 6 - 1

Chorus:

I SWEAR

Words and Music by
GARY BAKER and FRANK MYERS

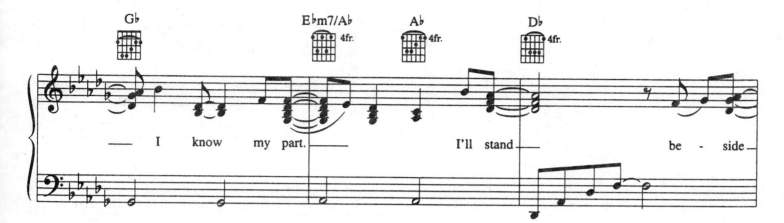

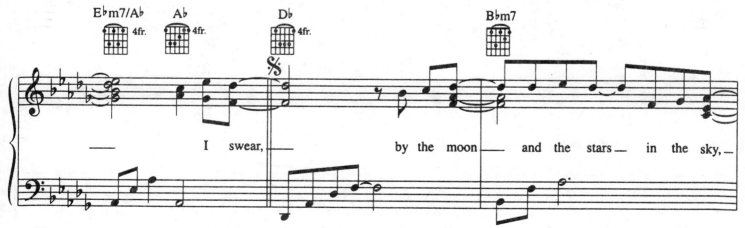

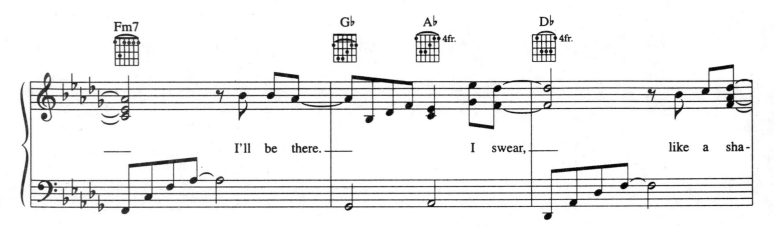

I'll be there. I swear, like a sha-

dow that's by your side, I'll be there. For

bet-ter or worse, till death do us part, I'll love you with ev - er - y beat.

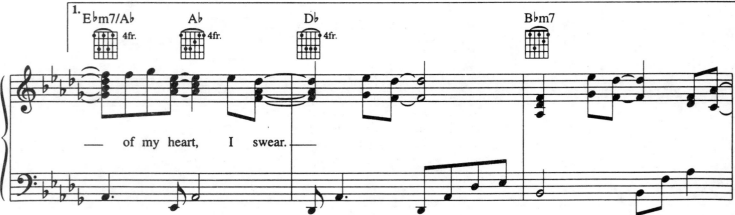

of my heart, I swear.

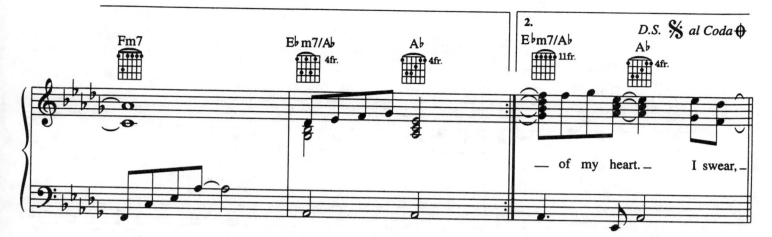

Additional lyrics

2. I'll give you everything I can,
I'll build your dreams with these two hands,
And we'll hang some memories on the wall.
And when there's silver in your hair,
You won't have to ask if I still care,
'Cause as time turns the page my love won't age at all.
(To Chorus)

I WILL ALWAYS LOVE YOU

Words and Music by
DOLLY PARTON

I Will Always Love You - 5 - 1

Verse 3: Instrumental solo

Verse 4:
I hope life treats you kind
And I hope you have all you've dreamed of.
And I wish to you, joy and happiness.
But above all this, I wish you love.
(To Chorus:)

IF IT MAKES YOU HAPPY

Words and Music by
SHERYL CROW and JEFF TROTT

If It Makes You Happy - 5 - 1

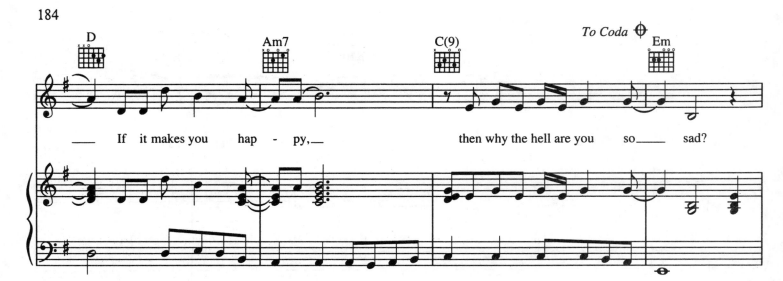

If it makes you hap - py, then why the hell are you so___ sad?

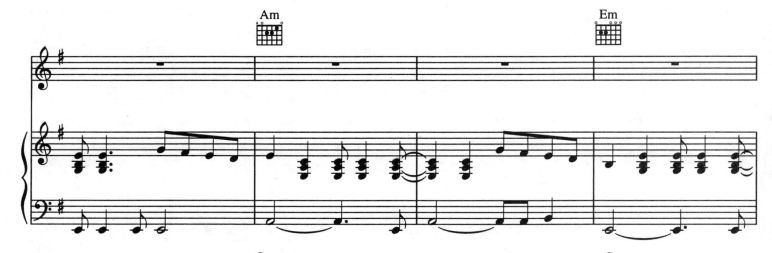

D.S. 𝄋 al Coda

3. We've been far,___

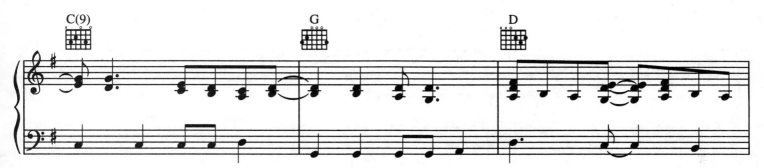

If It Makes You Happy - 5 - 5

I WILL COME TO YOU

Words and Music by
ISAAC HANSON, TAYLOR HANSON,
ZACHARY HANSON, BARRY MANN
and CYNTHIA WEIL

I Will Come to You - 6 - 1

some - one__ who'll al - ways__ un - der - stand._____

So if you feel that your soul is dy - ing, and you need the strength to keep try - ing,

I'll reach out__ and take__ your hand,__ oh._____

Na, na, na, na, na, na, na, na, na, na, na, na._____ I'll reach out for your

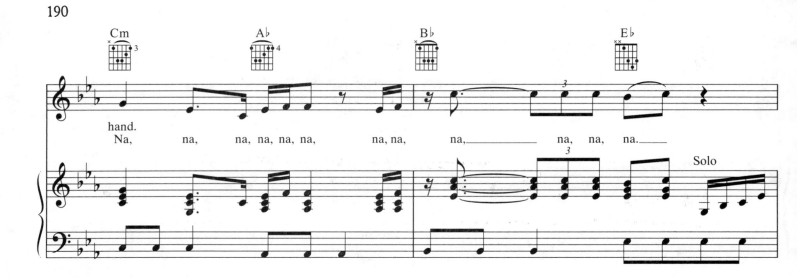

hand.
Na, na, na, na, na, na, na, na, na,_____ na, na, na._____

Solo

I'll come__ to

you,___ oh._____ When you have no light__ to guide you, and no

one to walk__ be-side__ you, I will come to you,__ oh,____ I will come_____

IF TOMORROW NEVER COMES

Words and Music by
GARTH BROOKS and KENT BLAZY

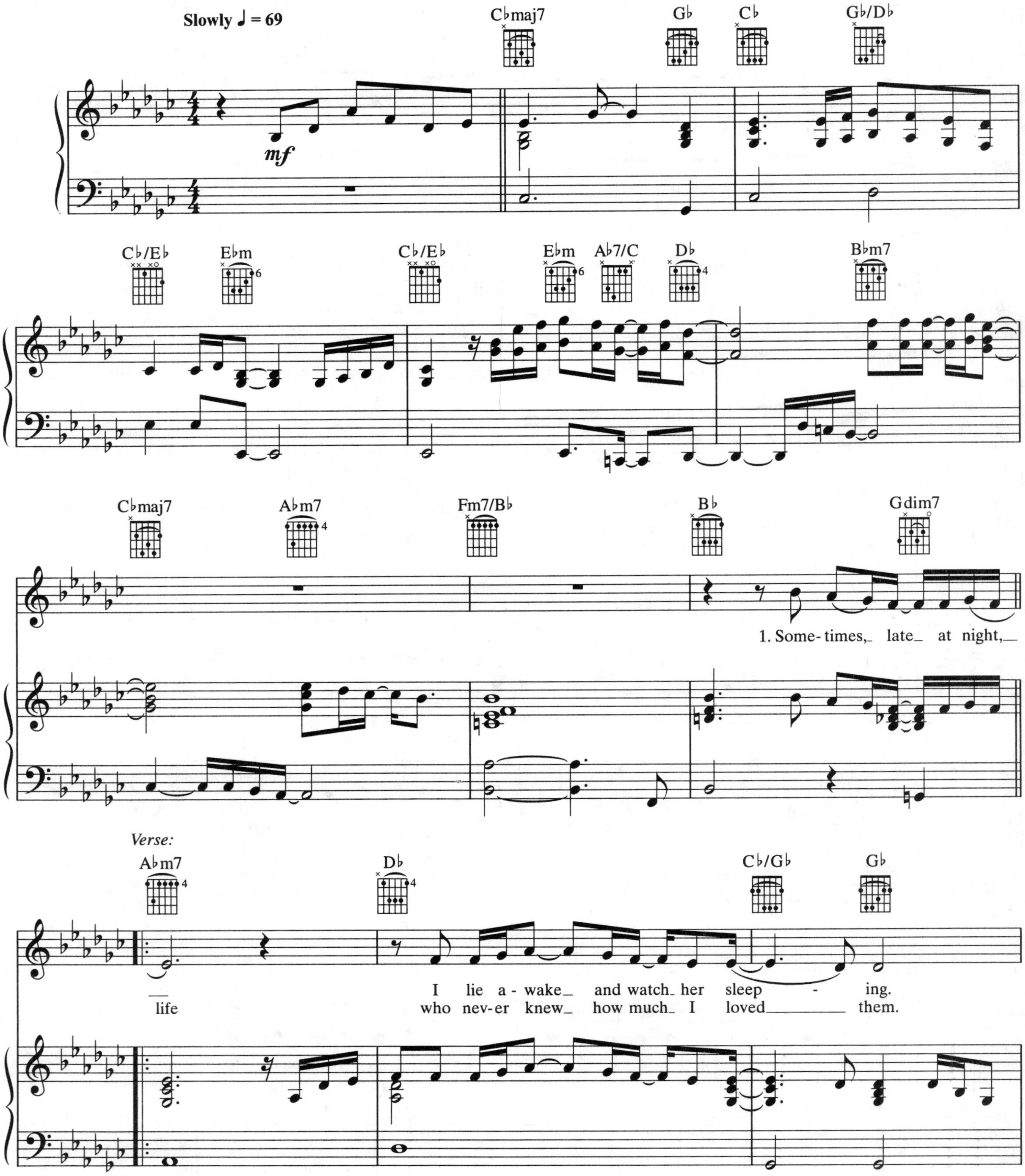

Slowly ♩ = 69

1. Some-times,_ late_ at night,_

Verse:

life

I lie a-wake_ and watch_ her sleep - ing.
who nev-er knew_ how much_ I loved_____ them.

If Tomorrow Never Comes - 5 - 1

LOVE WILL KEEP US ALIVE

Words and Music by
JIM CAPALDI, PETER VALE
and PAUL CARRACK

stand - ing,___ all a - lone___ a - gainst the world out - side.___
wor - ry,___ some - times you've just___ got to let it ride.___
found___ you,___ there's no more emp - ti - ness in - side.___

Love Will Keep Us Alive - 5 - 1

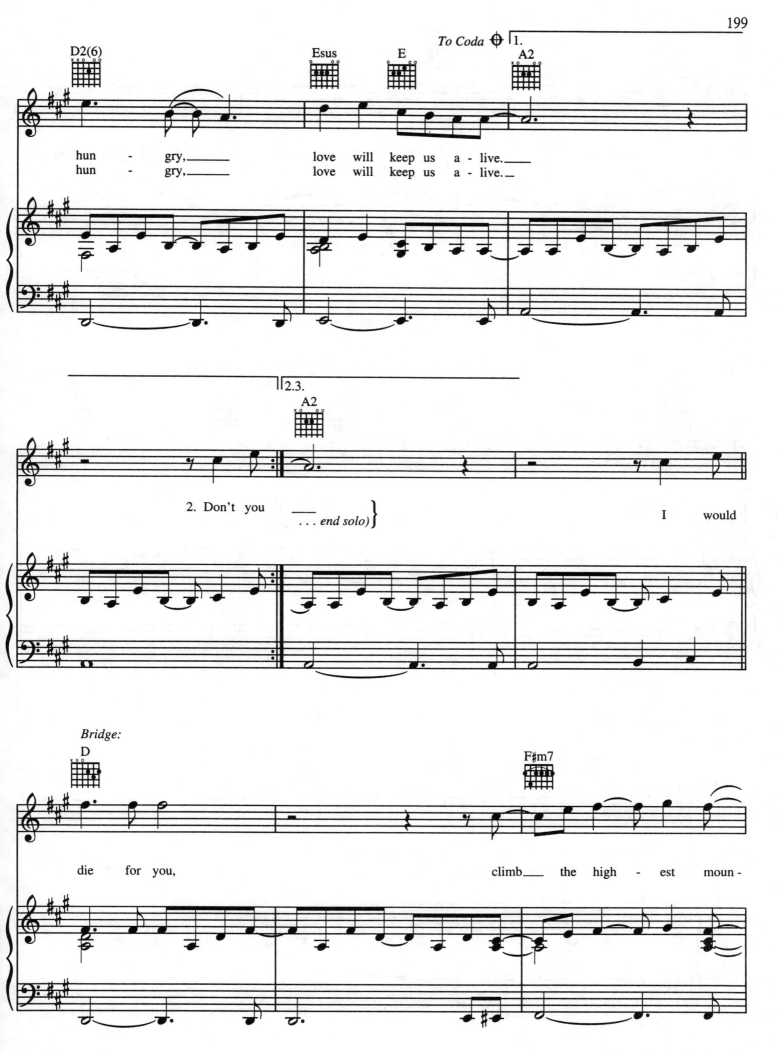

I'LL BE THERE FOR YOU
(Theme from "FRIENDS")

Words by
DAVID CRANE, MARTA KAUFFMAN, ALLEE WILLIS,
PHIL SOLEM and DANNY WILDE

Music by
MICHAEL SKLOFF

I'll Be There for You - 6 - 1

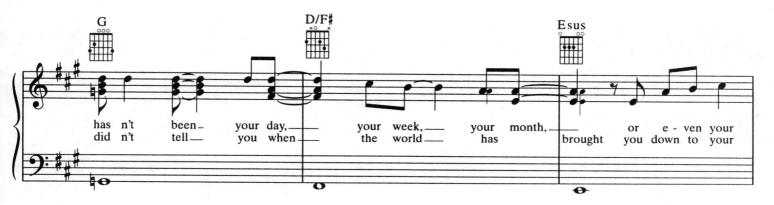

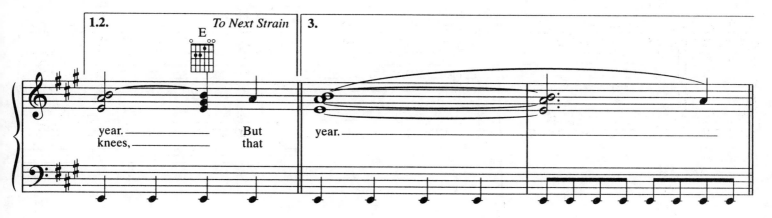

204

rain starts to pour. I'll be there for you

like I've been there be-fore. I'll be

there for you 'cause you're there for me,

too.

Guitar fill reads 8va.

I'll Be There for You - 6 - 3

Bridge:

No one could ev-

* Guitar fill reads 8va.

er know—me, no one could ev - er see—me.

Seems you're the on - ly one—who knows—— what it's

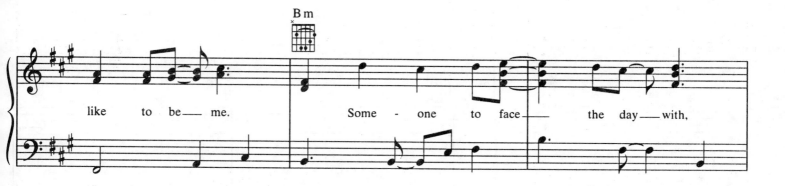

like to be—me. Some - one to face—— the day—with,

make it through all—— the rest—with, some - one I'll al -

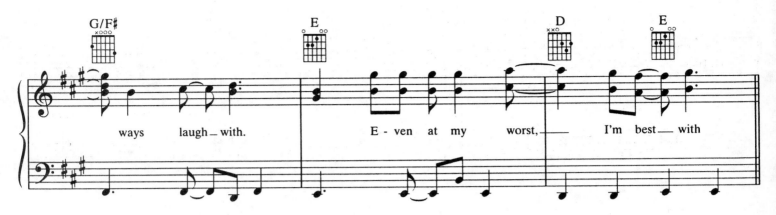

ways laugh — with. E - ven at my worst, — I'm best — with

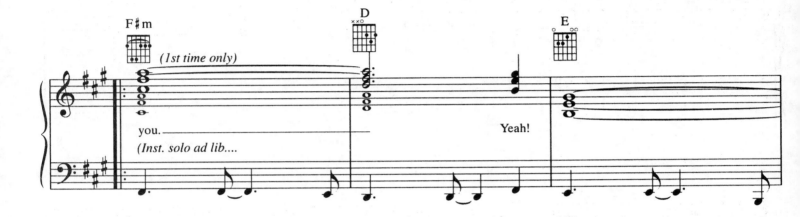

(1st time only)

you. _____ Yeah!

(Inst. solo ad lib....

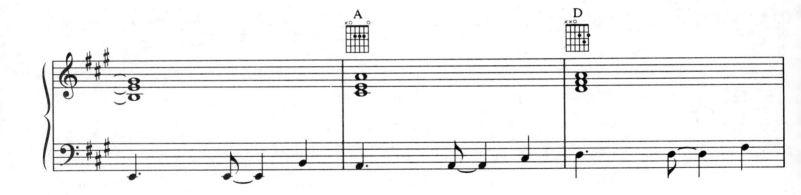

To Coda ⊕ **1.** **2.** *D.S. % al Coda*

...end solo)

KISS FROM A ROSE

Words and Music by
SEAL

Ba ya ya ba da ba da da da ba ya ya. Ba ya

ya ba da ba da da da ba ya ya. Ba ya da ba ya ya.

There___ used to be a grey-ing to-wer a - lone on the

sea. You___ be-came the light on the dark side of me.___ But love___ re-mains a

Kiss From a Rose - 6 - 1

drug that's the high and not the pill.__ But did you know that when it snows, my

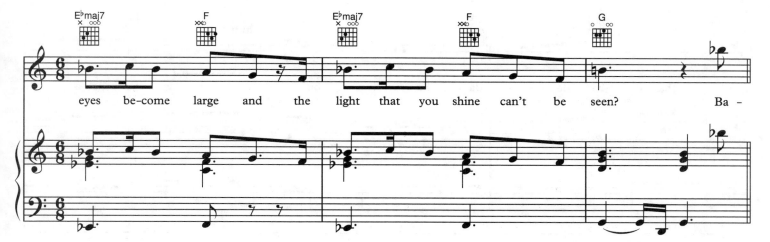

eyes be-come large and the light that you shine can't be seen? Ba -

-by,_____ I com - pare you to a kiss from a rose on the

grey. The more I get of you, the strang - er it feels, yeah._____ And now that your

rose is in bloom, a light hits the gloom on the grey.____ Ba ya

to Coda ⊕

ya ba da ba da da da ba ya ya. ba ya ya ba da ba da da

da ba ya ya. There is so much a man can tell you, so much he can

say.__ You__ re-main my pow-er, my pleas-ure, my pain. Ba-by,__ to

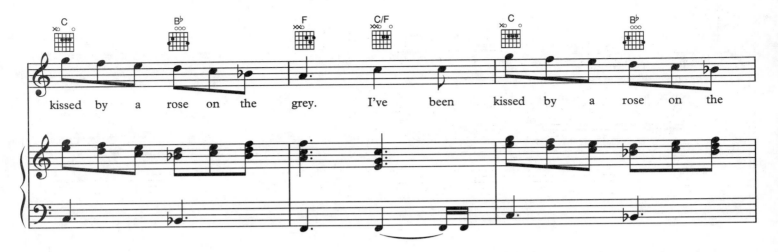

kissed by a rose on the grey. I've been kissed by a rose on the

grey. I've been kissed by a rose on the grey. I've been kissed by a rose on the

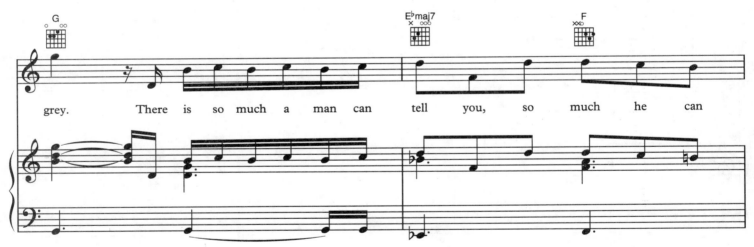

grey. There is so much a man can tell you, so much he can

say._ You re-main my pow-er, my pleas-ure, my pain. To

KISSING YOU
(Love Theme From "ROMEO + JULIET")

Words and Music by
DES'REE and TIM ATACK

Moderately slow ♩. = 112

1. Pride__ can stand a thou-sand tri-als, the strong__ will nev-er fall. But watch-ing stars__ with-out__ you, my__ soul cried._____

Kissing You - 4 - 1

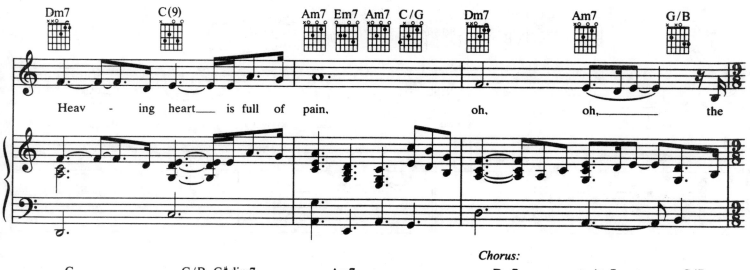

Heav - ing heart___ is full of pain, oh, oh,___ the

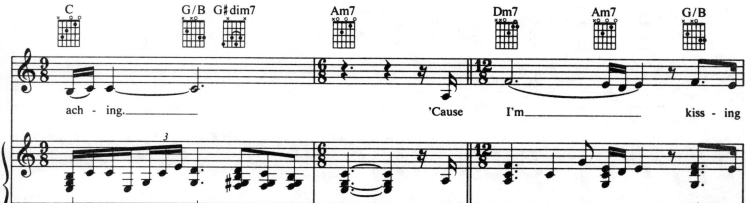

Chorus:

ach - ing.___ 'Cause I'm___ kiss - ing

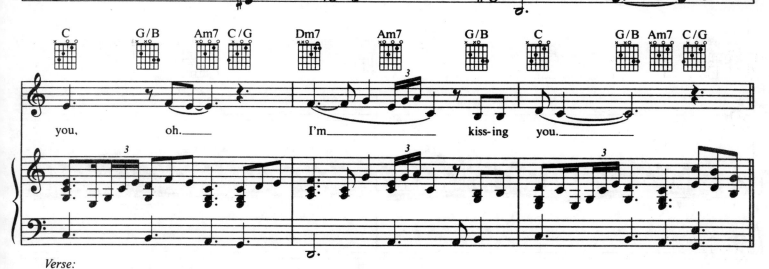

you, oh.___ I'm___ kiss-ing you.___

Verse:

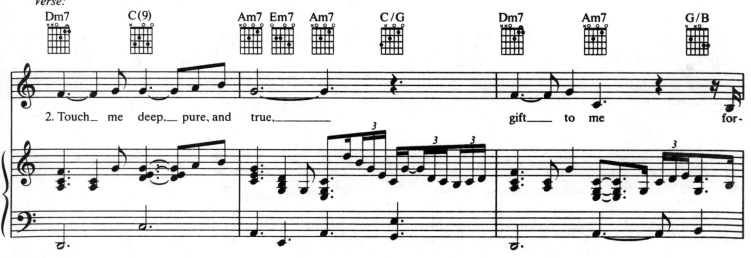

2. Touch__ me deep,__ pure, and true,___ gift___ to me for-

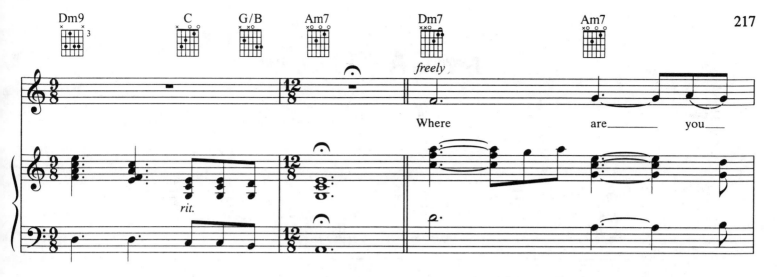

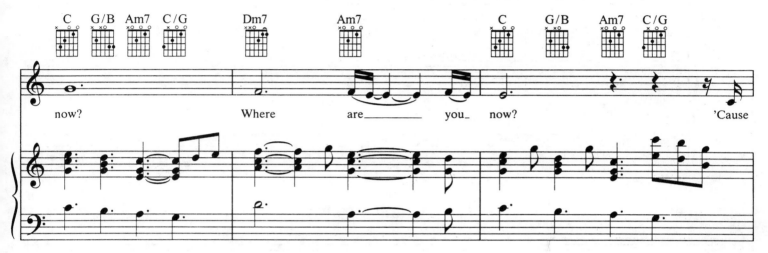

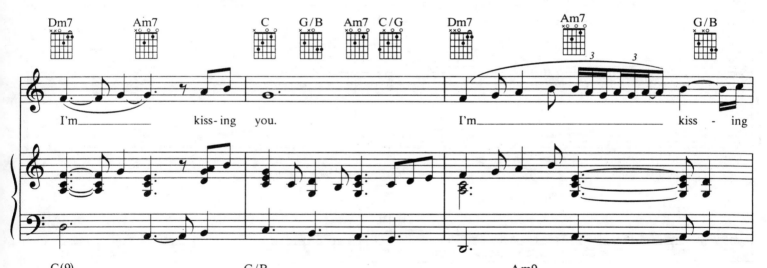

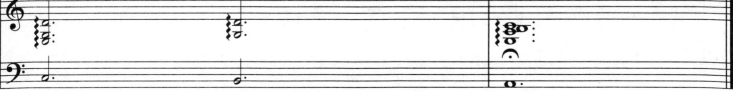

MACARENA

Words and Music by
ANTONIO ROMERO
and RAFAEL RUIZ

Coro:

Da - le a tu cuer - po a-le-grí - a Ma-ca-re-na que tu cuer-po_es pa' dar - le_a-le-grí-a y co-sa bue-na.

Macarena - 6 - 1

Da - le a tu cuer - po a - le - grí - a Ma - ca - re - na,   eh, _____ Ma - ca - re - na.

Verso 3:
Macarena sueña con el Corte inglés
Y se compra los modelos mas modernos.
Le gustaría vivir en Nueva York
Y ligar un novio nuevo.

Puente 2:
Macarena sueña con el Corte inglés
Y se compra los modelos mas modernos.
Le gustaría vivir en Nueva York
Y ligar un novio nuevo.
(Al Coro:)

Verso 4:
Macarena tiene un novio que se llama,
Que se llama de apellido Vitorino.
Y en la jura de bandera del muchacho
Se la dió con dos amigos.

Puente 3:
Macarena tiene un novio que se llama,
Que se llama de apellido Vitorino.
Y en la jura de bandera del muchacho
Se la dió con dos amigos.
(Al Coro:)

MISLED

Words and Music by
PETER ZIZZO and JIMMY BRALOWER

Misled - 5 - 1

226

Misled - 5 - 3

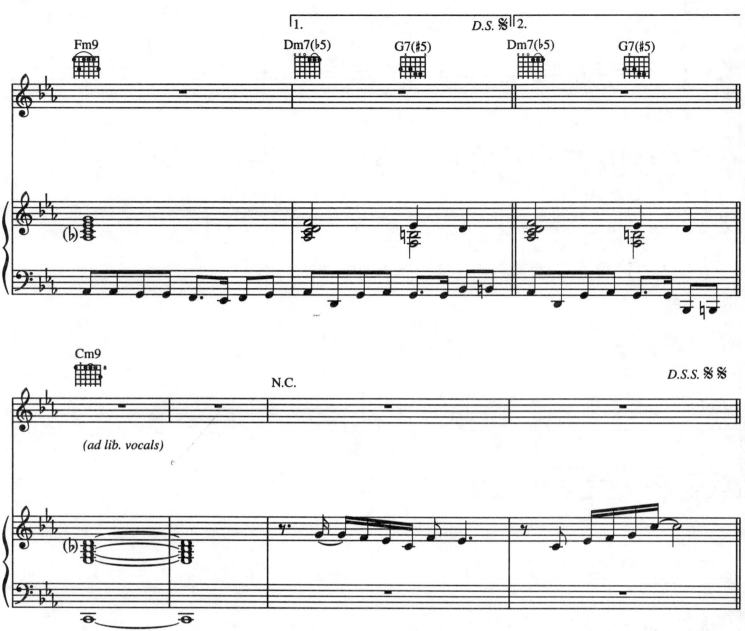

Verse 2:
Lovin' somebody ain't your average 9 to 5.
It takes conviction, it takes a will to survive.
I'm not somebody who commits the crime and leaves the scene.
But when I've been dissed, I don't spend much time on what might've been.

Bridges 2 & 3:
I'm not about self-pity, your love did me wrong,
So I'm movin', movin' on.
(To Chorus:)

MMMBOP

Words and Music by
ISAAC HANSON, TAYLOR HANSON
and ZAC HANSON

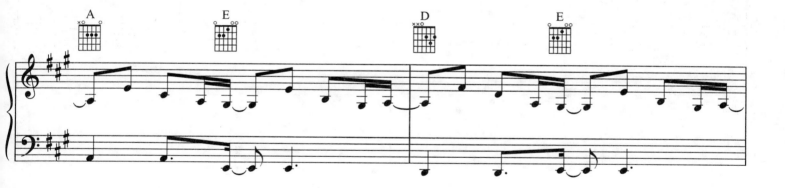

Mmmbop - 7 - 1

Verse:

1. You have so man-y re-la-tion-ships_ in this life, on-ly one or two_ will last._

_ You go through all the pain_ and strife,_ then you turn your back_ and they're gone so fast._

_ Oh yeah, and they're gone_

so_ fast, yeah._

MORE THAN WORDS

Lyrics and Music by
BETTENCOURT, CHERONE

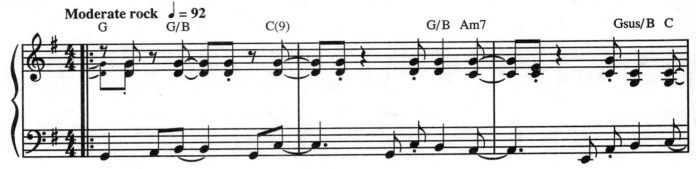

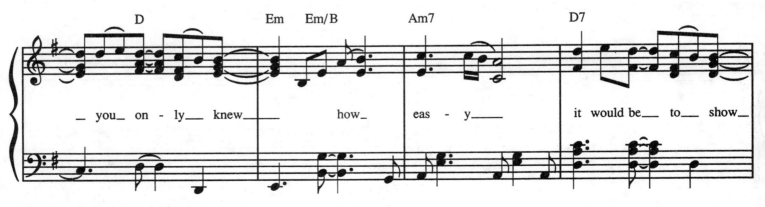

More Than Words - 4 - 1

_ me how_ you feel,_____ more than words_____ is all you have_ to___ do_

_ to make_ it___ real.____ Then, you would - n't have_ to say_____ that you love_

_ me,_____ 'cause I'd____ al - read - y_____ know.   What

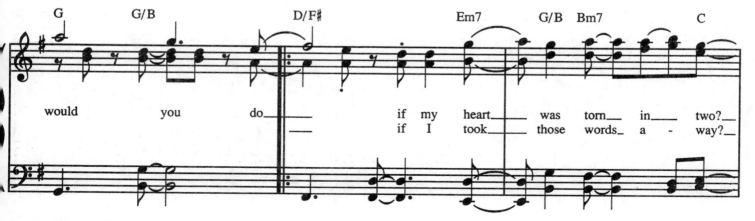

would   you   do___ ___   if my heart____ was torn__ in___ two?___
                                    ___ if I took____ those words_ a - way?___

Verse 2:
Now that I have tried to talk to you
And make you understand.
All you have to do is close your eyes
And just reach out your hands.
And touch me, hold me close, don't ever let me go.
More than words is all I ever needed you to show.
Then you wouldn't have to say
That you love me 'cause I'd already know.
(To Chorus:)

MUSTANG SALLY

Words and Music by
BONNY RICE

Moderate rock ♩ = 120

Mus-tang Sal -

Verse:

ly, guess you bet-ter slow that Mus-tang down._

Mus-tang

Sal-ly, now ba - by, guess you bet-ter slow that Mus-tang down._

Mustang Sally - 4 - 1

— You been

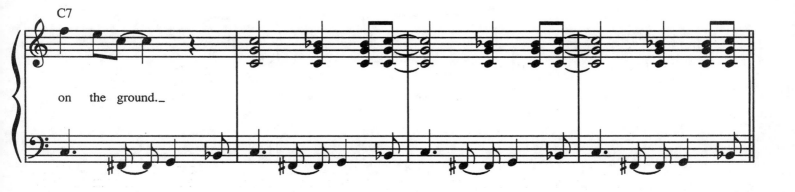

run-nin' all___ o - ver town,___ ooh,___ I guess you got-ta put your flat feet

on the ground.___

Chorus:

All you wan-na do is ride___ a-round, Sal-ly. (Ride, Sal-ly,___ ride.___)

242

Mustang Sally - 4 - 3

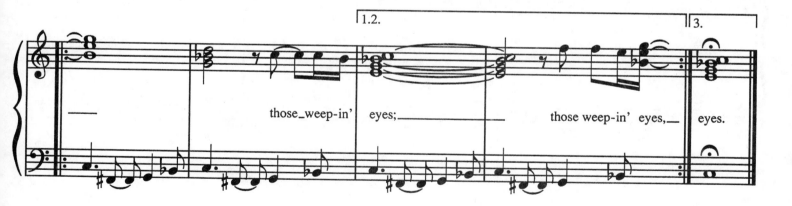

Verse 2:
I bought you a brand new Mustang,
It was a nineteen sixty five.
Now you come around, signifying a woman.
Girl, you won't, you won't let me ride.
Mustang Sally, now baby,
Guess you better slow that Mustang down.
You been runnin' all over town.
Oh, guess you gotta put your flat feet on the ground.
(To Chorus:)

NOW AND FOREVER

Music and Lyrics by
RICHARD MARX

Slowly ♩ = 80

(with pedal)

Verse:

1. When - ev - er I'm wear - y___ from the bat - tles that rage in my
2. Some - times I just hold you,___ too caught up in me to

head, you make sense of I'm hold - ing a mad - ness when my for - tune that
see

san - i - ty hangs by a thread. I lose my way,___
heav - en has giv - en to me. I'll try to show___

Now and Forever - 4 - 1

but still you seem to un - der - stand.
you each and ev - 'ry way I can,
Now and for - ev -
now and for - ev -

- er,
- er,
I will be your man.
I will be your man.

Bridge:

Now I can rest my wor - ries and

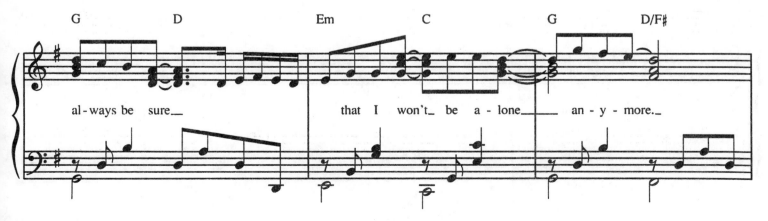

al - ways be sure that I won't be a - lone an - y - more.

If I'd on-ly known____ you were there____ all the time,____ all this time.____

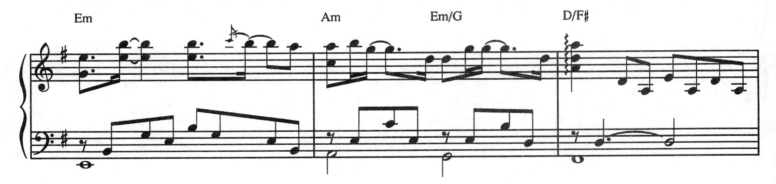

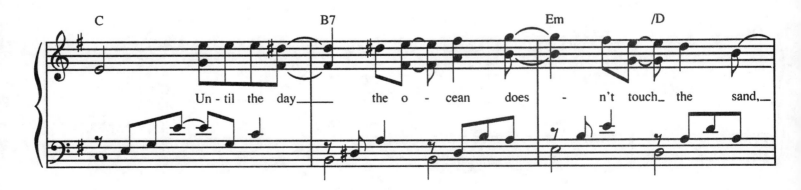

Un - til the day____ the o - cean does - n't touch____ the sand,

now and for ev - er.   I will be___ your man.___

Now and for - ev - er,

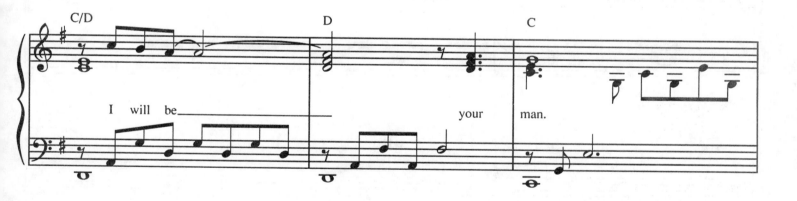

I will be___   your man.

poco rit. e dim.

mp

ONCE IN A LIFETIME

Words and Music by
WALTER AFANASIEFF, MICHAEL BOLTON
and DIANE WARREN

1.Some peo-ple fill their lives with emp-ty nights and days that slip a-way.

2.Some peo-ple live their lives in com-pro-mise and hide their dreams a-way.

Once in a Lifetime - 6 - 1

250

life - time.

If you be - lieve____ in the pow - er of love,____

then you be - lieve that dreams__ come true.____ Mag - ic will fill your heart____ when that

mo - ment comes a - long____ just once in your life.

Once in a

ONE OF US

Words and Music by
ERIC BAZILIAN

One of Us - 5 - 2

QUIT PLAYING GAMES
(With My Heart)

Words and Music by
MAX MARTIN and HERBERT CRICHLOW

1. Ev- en in my heart,____

(Verse 2 see block

I____ see

you're not be- in' true to me.____ deep with- in my soul____ I____

Quit Playing Games - 5 - 1

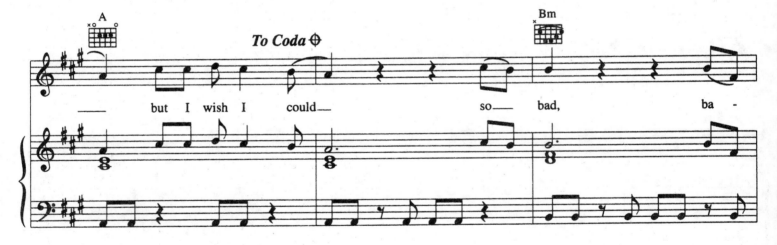

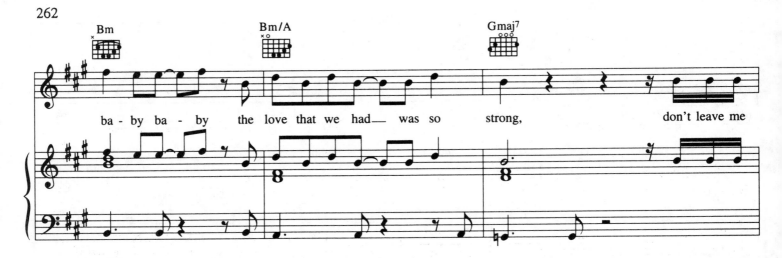

baby baby the love that we had____ was so strong, don't leave me

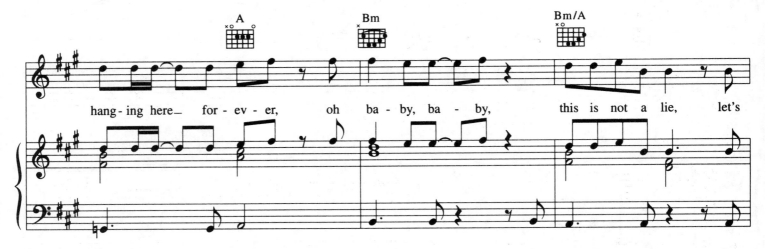

hang-ing here____ for-ev-er, oh ba-by, ba-by, this is not a lie, let's

D.%. al Coda

stop this to-night._____

Coda

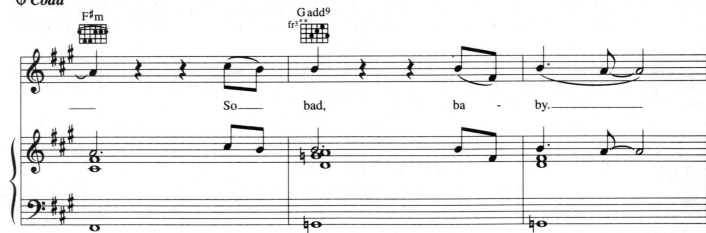

So____ bad, ba - by._____

Verse 2:
I live my life the way,
To keep you comin' back to me.
Everything I do is for you,
So what is it that you can't see?
Sometimes I wish I could turn back time,
Impossible as it may seem.
But I wish I could so bad, baby
You better quit playing games with my heart.

RETURN OF THE MACK

Words and Music by
PHIL CHILL and MARK MORRISON

Return of the Mack - 4 - 1

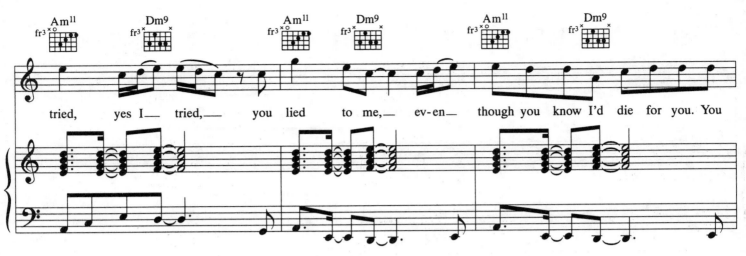

tried, yes I tried, you lied to me, ev-en though you know I'd die for you. You

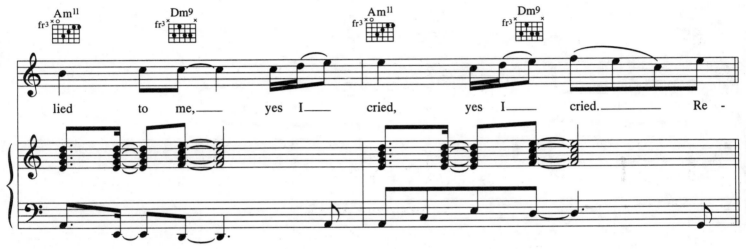

lied to me, yes I cried, yes I cried. Re -

turn of the mack, re - turn of the mack, re -
(here it is) (come on)

turn of the mack, you know that I'll be back. Re -
(oh my God) (here I am)

turn of — the mack,— re - turn of — the mack,— re - turn of — the mack,— you
(once again) (pump up the world) (watch my flow)

1. **2.**

know that I'll— back.— 2. So I know that I'll— be back.—
(here I go)

D.%.to fade

You

Verse 2:

So I'm back in the game
Running things to keep my swing
Letting all the people know
That I'm back to run the show
Cos what you did you know was wrong
And all the nasty things you've done
So baby listen carefully
While I sing my comeback song.

You lied to me
Cos she said she'd never turn on me
You lied to me
But you did, but you did
You lied to me
But I do, but I do, do do.

Return of the Mack
    Here it is
Return of the Mack
    Hold on
Return of the Mack
    Don't you know
You know that I'll be back
    Here I go
Return of the Mack
    Oh little girl
Return of the Mack
    Wants my pearl
Return of the Mack
    Up and down
You now that I'll be back
    Round and round.

D.%.

You lied to me
Cos she said she'd never turn on me
You lied to me
But you did, but you did
You lied to me
All these things you said I'd never do
You lied to me
But I do, but I do, do, do.

SAID I LOVED YOU . . . BUT I LIED

Composed by MICHAEL BOLTON
and ROBERT JOHN "MUTT" LANGE

Said I Loved You . . . But I Lied - 5 - 1

Shine your light on this heart of mine_____ till the end_____ of

this taste of heav-en so deep, so true._____ I've__ found__ in

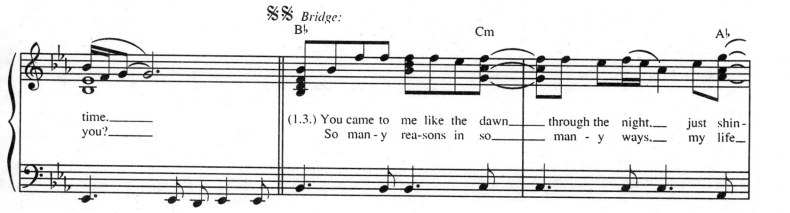

§§ Bridge:

time._____ (1.3.) You came to me like the dawn_____ through the night.__ just shin-

you?_____ So man-y rea-sons in so_____ man-y ways,__ my life__

- in' like__ the__ sun._____ Out of my dreams__ and

_____ has just__ be-gun._____ Need you for-ev-er, I

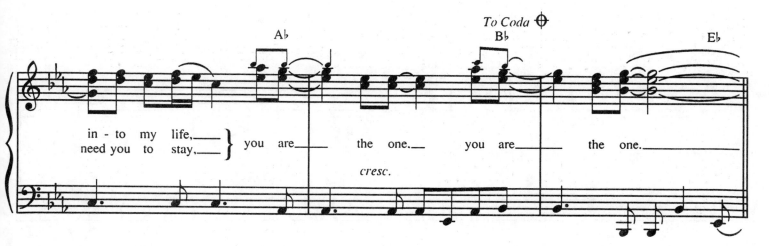

To Coda ⊕

in - to my life,_____ you are_____ the one.__ you are_____ the one._____

need you to stay,_____

cresc.

Said I Loved You . . . But I Lied - 5 - 2

Chorus:

Said I____ loved you, but I lied,

'cause this is more than love_ I feel____ in - side.____ Said I____ loved you, but I was

wrong,____ 'cause love could nev - er, ev - er feel____ so strong.____

Said I loved you, but I____ lied.____

dim.

mp

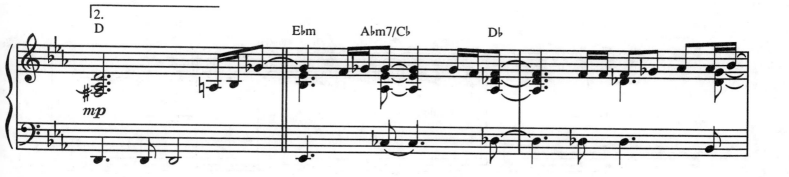

the one.

Said I____ loved you, but I lied, 'cause this is more than love___ I

feel___ in - side.___ Said I___ loved you, but I was wrong,___

'cause love could nev - er, ev - er feel___ so strong.___ Said I loved_ you,___

'cause this is more than love_ I feel___ in - side.___

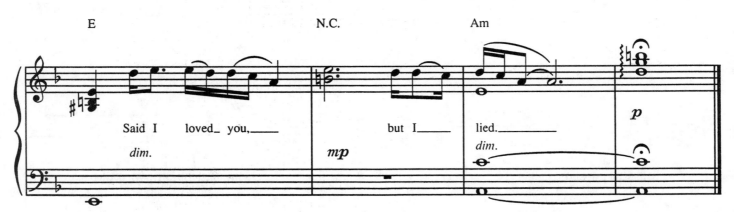

Said I loved_ you,___ but I___ lied.___

dim. mp dim. p

SAY YOU'LL BE THERE

Words and Music by
SPICE GIRLS and
ELIOT KENNEDY

Oh say you'll be there I'm giv-ing you eve-ry-thing— all that joy—

——can bring— this I swear.——   1. Last time

Say You'll Be There - 5 - 1

that we had— this con-ver-sa-tion I de-ci - ded we should be friends,——— yeah.

But now we're go-ing round— in cir-cles tell me will this dé-jà vu nev-er end—

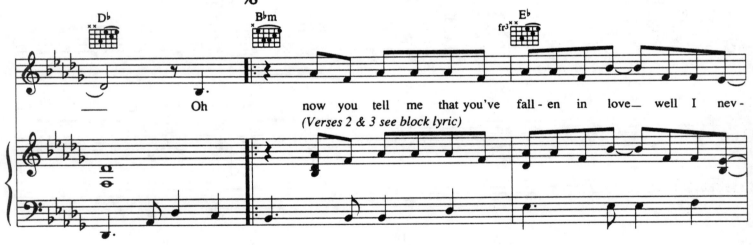

Oh now you tell me that you've fall-en in love— well I nev-
(Verses 2 & 3 see block lyric)

- er ev - er thought that would be,——— yeah. This time you

Repeat to fade

Verse 2:

If you put two and two together you will see what our friendship is for,
If you can't work this equation then I guess I'll have to show you the door,
There is no need to say you love me it would be better left unsaid.

I'm giving you everything all that joy can bring this I swear,
And all that I want from you is a promise you will be there,
Yeah I want you.

Verse 3: *(Instrumental)*
Any fool can see they're falling, gotta make you understand.
To Coda

SAND AND WATER

Words and Music by
BETH NIELSEN CHAPMAN

Moderately ♩ = 112

(with pedal)

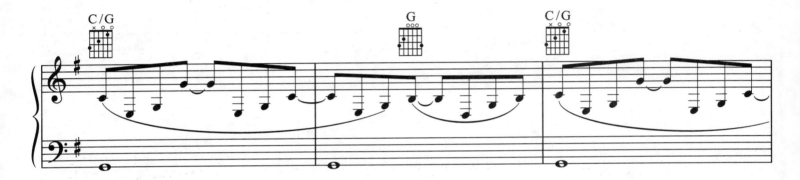

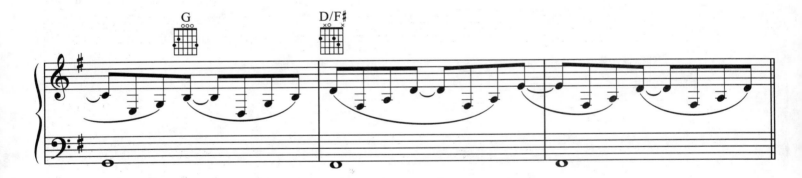

𝄋 *Verse:*

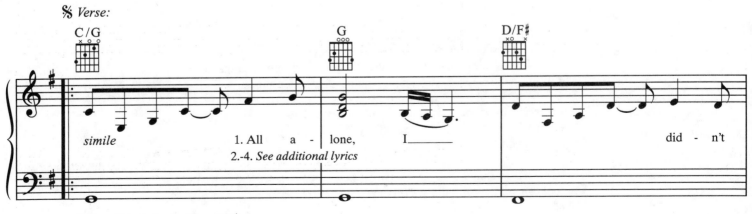

simile

1. All a - lone, I____ did - n't

2.-4. *See additional lyrics*

*Recording is in the key of F♯.

Sand and Water - 4 - 1

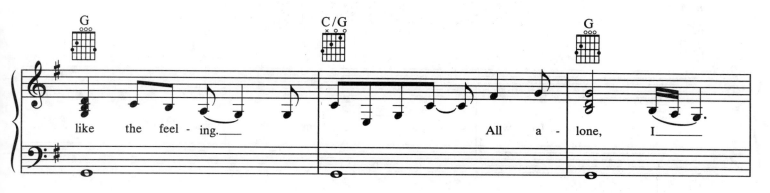

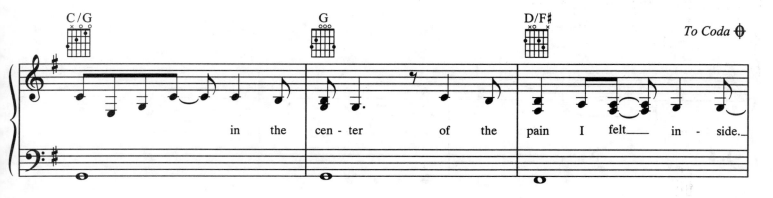

Sand and Water - 4 - 2

Chorus:

I will see you_____ in the light of_____ a thou-

sand suns._ I will hear you_____ in the

sound_____ of the waves. I will

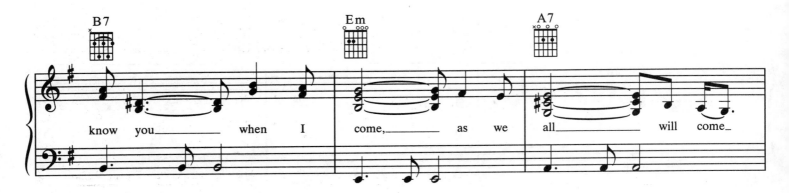

know you_____ when I come,_____ as we all_____ will come_

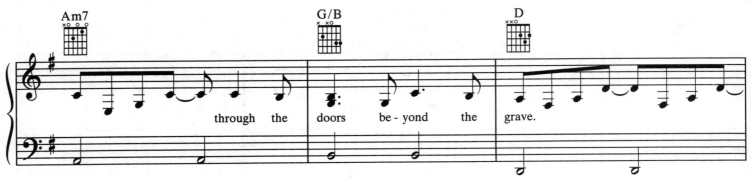

through the doors be-yond the grave.

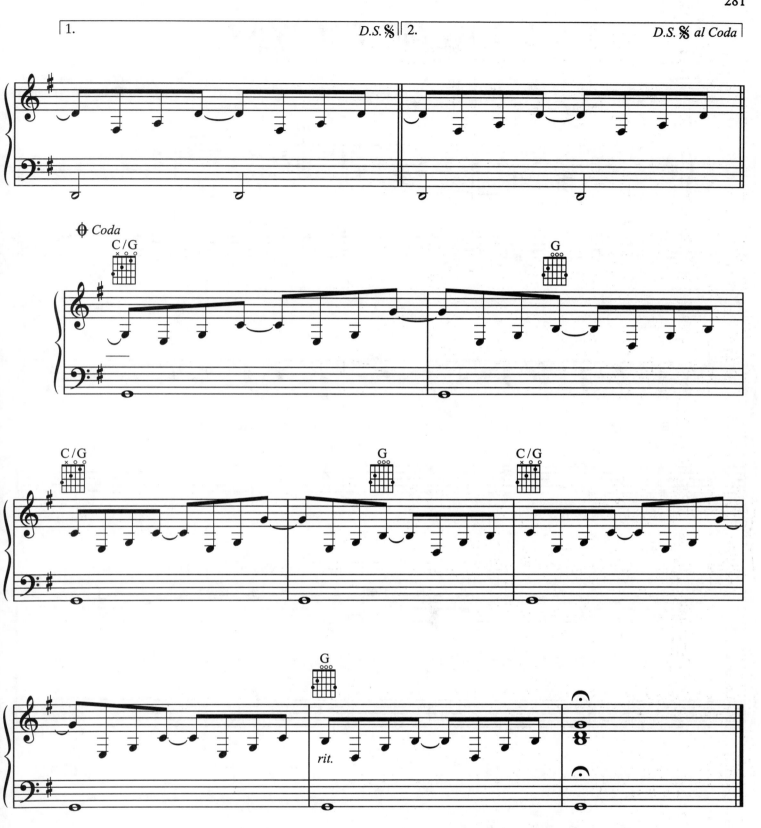

Verses 2 & 4:
All alone I came into this world,
All alone I will someday die.
Solid stone is just sand and water, baby,
Sand and water and a million years gone by.
(To Chorus/Coda:)

Verse 3:
All alone I heal this heart of sorrow,
All alone I raise this child.
Flesh and bone, he's just bursting towards tomorrow,
And his laughter fills my world and wears your smile.
(To Chorus:)

SHOW ME THE WAY

Lyrics and Music by
DENNIS DE YOUNG

Ev - 'ry night I say a pray'r in the hopes that there's a heav - en.___ But

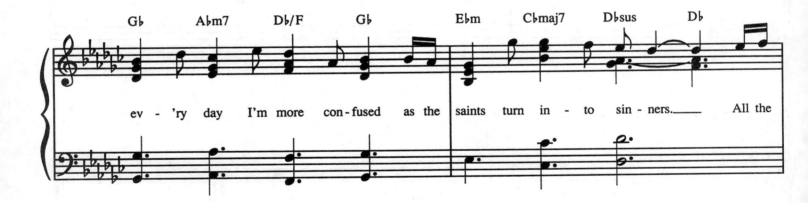

ev - 'ry day I'm more con - fused as the saints turn in - to sin - ners.___ All the

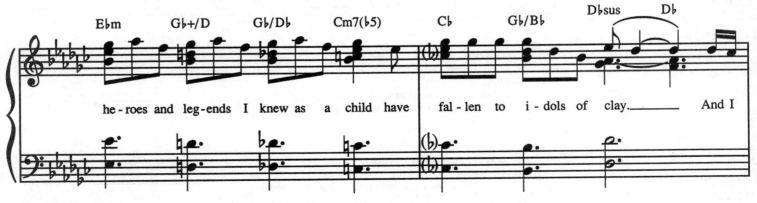

he - roes and leg - ends I knew as a child have fal - len to i - dols of clay.___ And I

Show Me the Way - 4 - 1

strength and the cour-age to be-lieve that I'll get there some day.____ And please show me the

way.

mf

mp *Slower*

p

Ev - 'ry night I say a pray'r in the hopes that there's a heav-en.____

Verse 2:
And as I slowly drift to sleep
For a moment dreams are sacred.
I close my eyes and know there's peace
In a world so filled with hatred.
Then I wake up each morning and turn on the news
To find we've so far to go.
And I keep on hoping for a sign
So afraid I just won't know.
(To Chorus:)

SO HELP ME GIRL

Words and Music by
HOWARD PERDEW and ANDY SPOONER

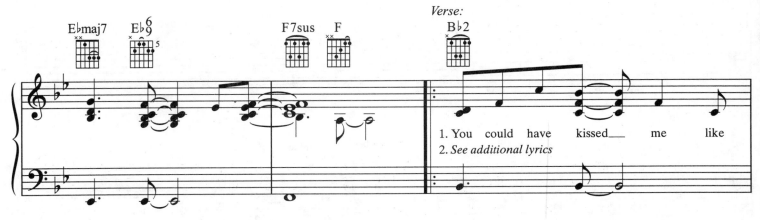

So Help Me Girl - 4 - 1

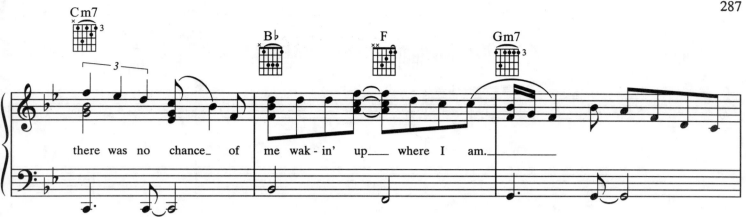

there was no chance___ of me wak-in' up___ where I am.___

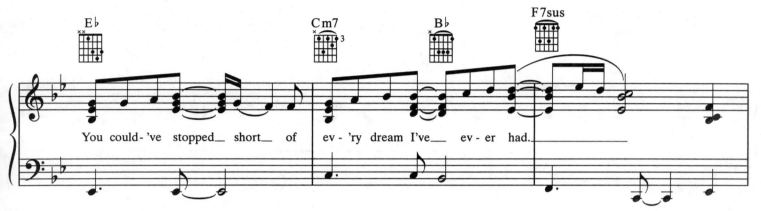

You could-'ve stopped___ short___ of ev-'ry dream I've___ ev-er had.___

% *Chorus:*

So help___ me, girl,___ you've gone___ too far.___ It's way___ too late___

___ to save___ my heart. The way___ it feels___ each time___ we touch,

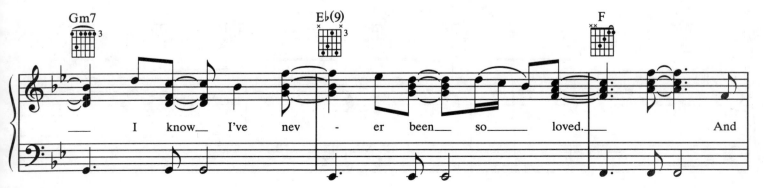

___ I know___ I've nev - er been so___ loved.___ And

So Help Me Girl - 4 - 2

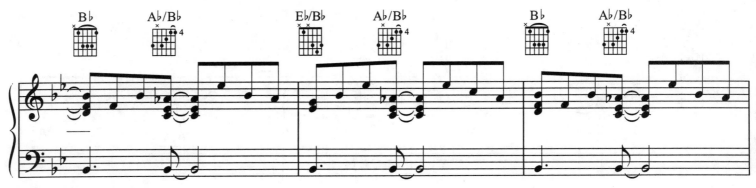

Fall - in', fall - in', fall - in', fall...
You've got me fall - in'

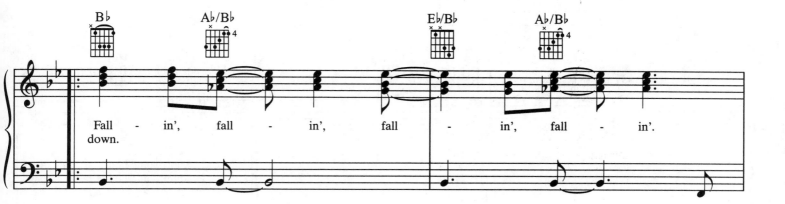

Fall - in', fall - in', fall - in', fall - in'.
down.

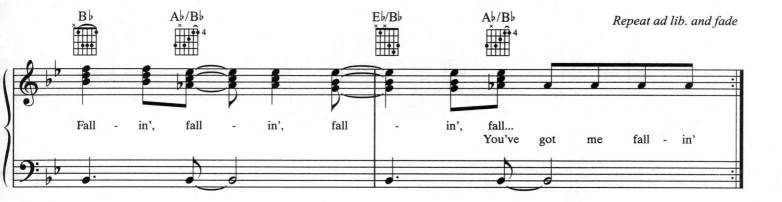

Repeat ad lib. and fade

Fall - in', fall - in', fall - in', fall...
You've got me fall - in'

Verse 2:
You had to be there until the song came on,
Makin' last night feel like a vision of things yet to come.
You just start to hold me like nobody else.
Look what you've gone and done.
You had to love me till I just can't get enough.
(To Chorus:)

SOMEBODY'S CRYING

Words and Music by
CHRIS ISAAK

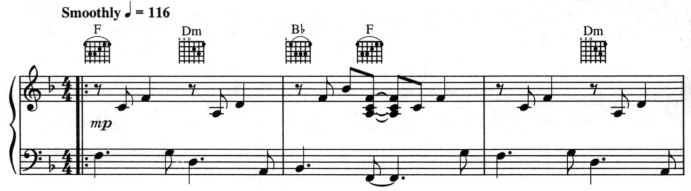

1. I know some-bod - y   and they
2. I know some-bod - y   and they
3. Give me   a   sign and let me

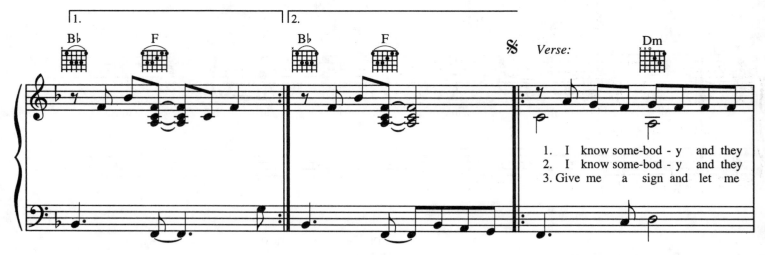

cry   for you.___ They lie a - wake at night and dream of you.___ I bet you nev - er e - ven
called your name___ a mil-lion times and still you nev - er came.___ They go on lov-ing you
know we're through,___ if you don't love me   like I love you.___ But if you cry at night the

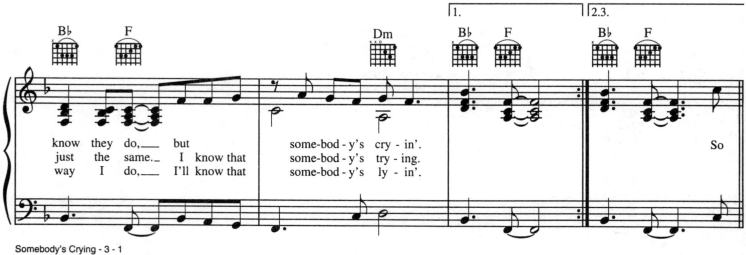

know they do,___ but   some-bod - y's cry - in'.
just the   same.___ I know that some-bod - y's try - ing.
way I   do,___ I'll know that some-bod - y's ly - in'.   So

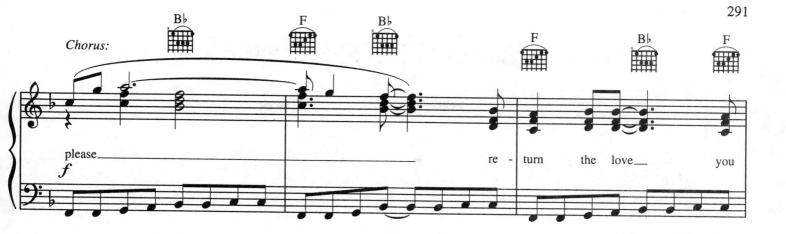

Chorus:

please_____ re - turn the love__ you

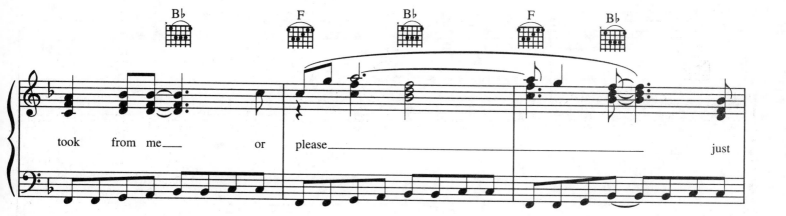

took from me__ or please_____ just

let me know__ if it can't be me.__ I know when some-bod - y's ly - in'.

To Coda $\oplus$

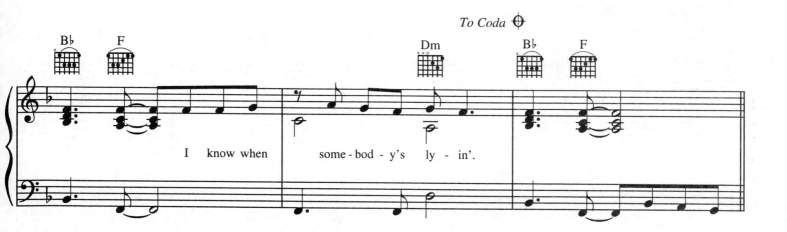

I know when some-bod - y's ly - in'.

STREETS OF PHILADELPHIA

Words and Music by
BRUCE SPRINGSTEEN

Moderately, with a beat ♩ = 96

Verse:

bruised and bat-tered; I could-n't __ tell __ what I felt. I was __ un-rec-og-niz - a-ble __ to my-

self. Saw my re-flec-tion in a win-dow and did-n't know my own face. __ Oh, broth-er are you

Chorus:

gon-na leave me wast-in' a - way on the streets of Phil-a- del-phi-a. __

(bkgrd.) La __ la la la la

(L.H. cue notes 2nd & 3rd time)

Streets of Philadelphia - 3 - 1

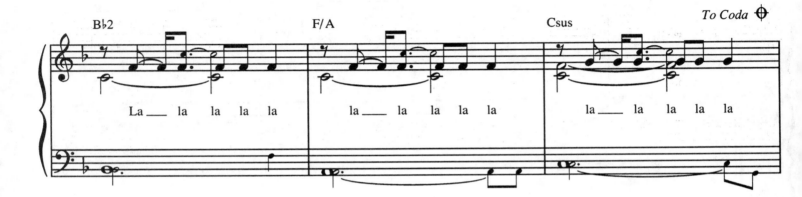

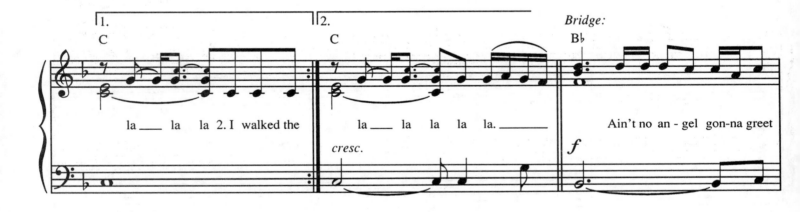

And my clothes don't fit me no more;__ I walked a thou-sand miles __ just to __

D.S. %S al Coda

⊕ *Coda*

__slip this skin. _

la __ la la la la. ____

1.2. La __ la la la la
3.4.(etc.) *Instrumental repeat & fade*

Repeat ad lib. and fade

la __ la la la la

la __ la la la la

la __ la la la la. __

Verse 2:
I walked the avenue till my legs felt like stone.
I heard the voices of friends vanished and gone.
At night I could hear the blood in my veins
Just as black and whispering as the rain
On the streets of Philadelphia.
(To Chorus:)

Verse 3:
The night has fallen. I'm lyin' awake.
I can feel myself fading away.
So, receive me, brother, with your faithless kiss,
Or will we leave each other alone like this
On the streets of Philadelphia?
(To Chorus:)

SOMEBODY BIGGER THAN YOU AND I

Words and Music by
JOHNNY LANGE, HY HEATH
and SONNY BURKE

Somebody Bigger Than You and I - 2 - 1

SOMETHING ABOUT THE WAY
YOU LOOK TONIGHT

Lyrics by
BERNIE TAUPIN

Music by
ELTON JOHN

Something About the Way You Look Tonight - 4 - 1

From the Lucasfilm Ltd. Productions "STAR WARS", "THE EMPIRE STRIKES BACK" and "RETURN OF THE JEDI" - Twentieth Century-Fox Releases.

STAR WARS
(Main Theme)

Music by
JOHN WILLIAMS

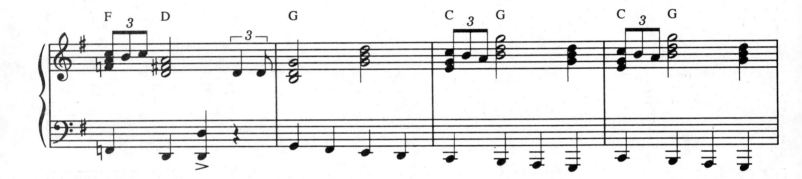

Star Wars (Main Theme) - 2 - 1

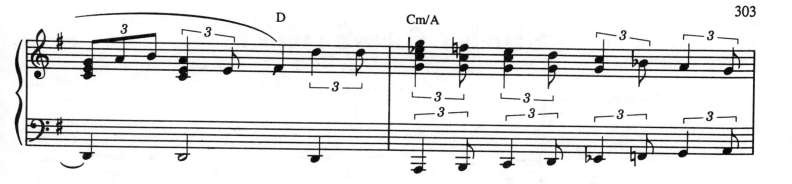

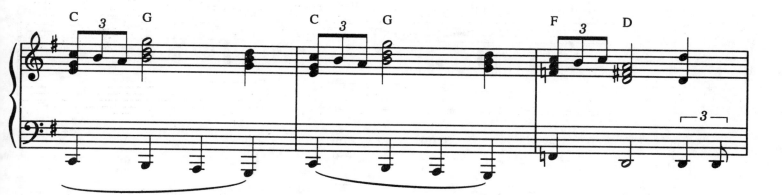

SUNNY CAME HOME

Words and Music by
SHAWN COLVIN and JOHN LEVENTHAL

Verse 1:

1. Sun-ny came home to her fa-v'rite room._ Sun-ny sat down in the

Sunny Came Home - 6 - 1

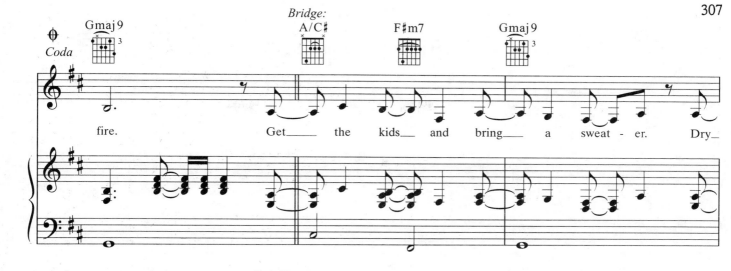

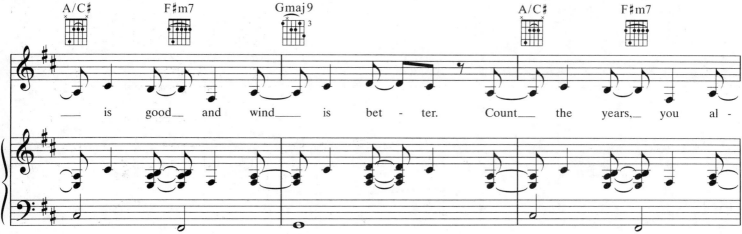

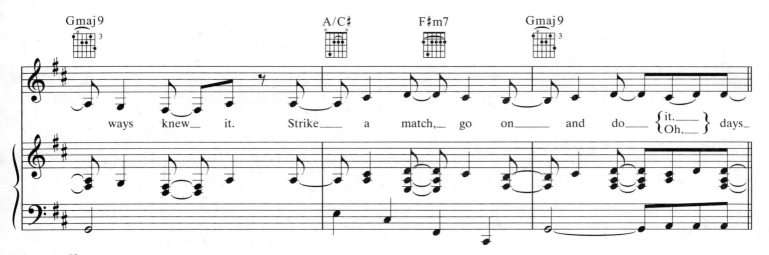

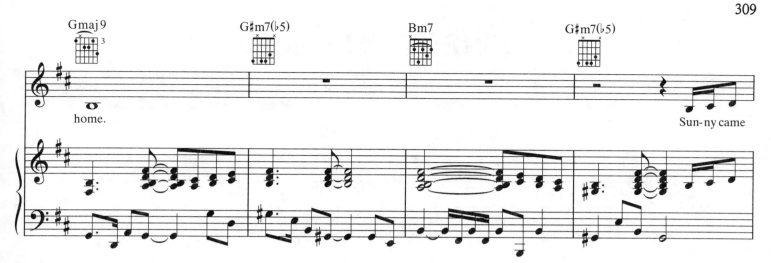

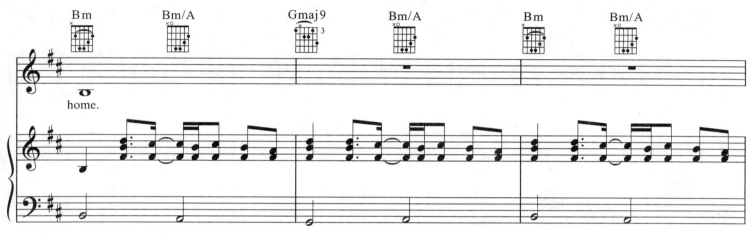

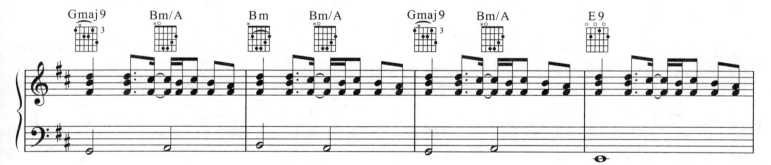

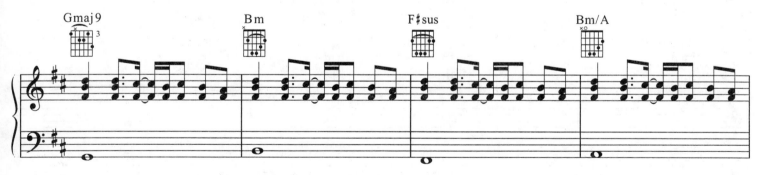

SWEET DREAMS

Words and Music by
GERD AMIR SARAF, MEHMET SOENMEZ,
ROBERT HAYNES and MELANIE THORNTON

Dance rock ♩ = 126

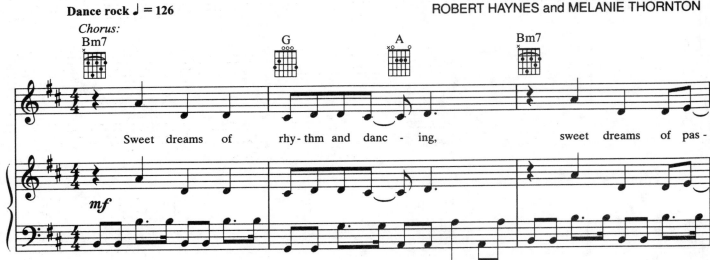

Sweet dreams of rhythm and dancing, sweet dreams of pas-

-sion through the night. Sweet dreams are taking over,

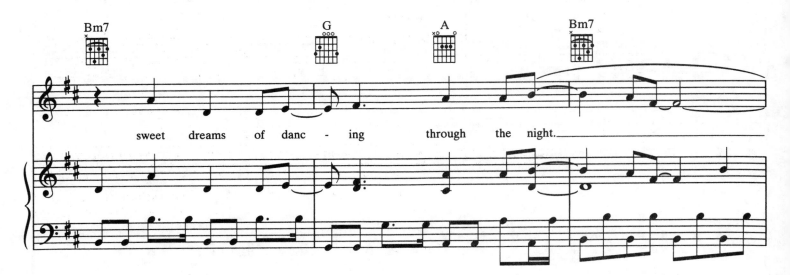

sweet dreams of dancing through the night.

Sweet Dreams - 6 - 1

Lyrics:
1. I wan-na get in-to mo - tion, a bet-ter de-vo - tion, so I can
2. Rhy-thm is a cre-a - tion, a bet-ter sen-sa - tion, that will

make it through_ the night. So the mu-sic is play - ing, you know what I'm say-
lead you through_ the night. When your bod-y is mov - ing, the mu-sic is groov-

Chorus:

-ing, now ev-'ry-thing will be al-right.
-ing, I wan-na take you home to-night.
Sweet dreams of

rhy-thm and danc-ing, sweet dreams of pas-sion through the night.

Sweet dreams are tak-ing o-ver, sweet dreams of danc-

-ing through the night.

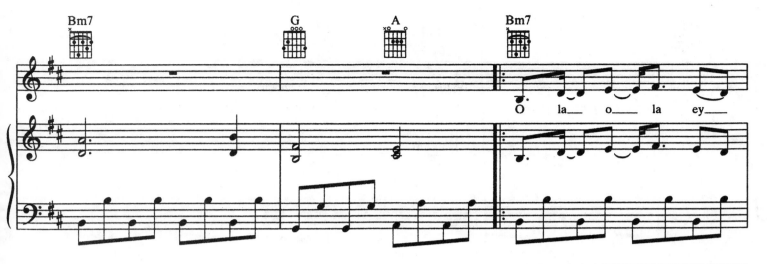

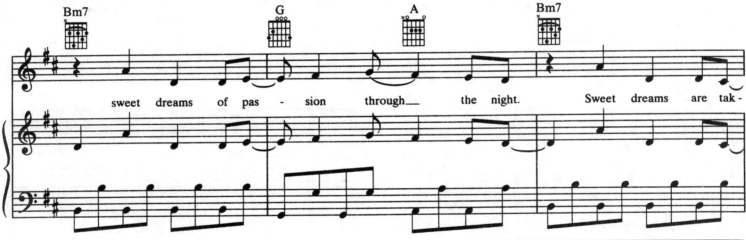

THE SWEETEST DAYS

Words and Music by
WENDY WALDMAN, JON LIND
and PHIL GALDSTON

You and I in this mo — ment hold-in' the night__ so__
There are times that scare_____ me. You rat-tle the house_ like the

close;_____ hang-in' on, still un-bro - ken, while
wind._____ Both of us so un-bend - ing, we

The Sweetest Days - 4 - 1

(These are the days.) Ev-'ry day is the sweet-est day we'll know; (These are the days.

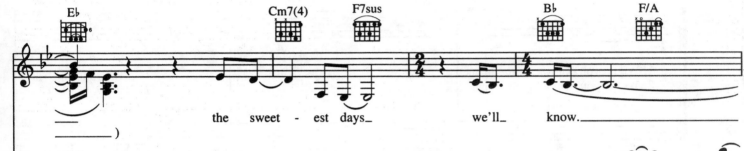

the sweet-est days we'll know.

poco rit. e dim. *p*

The Sweetest Days - 4 - 4

TEARS IN HEAVEN

Moderately slow ♩ = 80

Words and Music by
WILL JENNINGS and ERIC CLAPTON

Tears in Heaven - 4 - 1

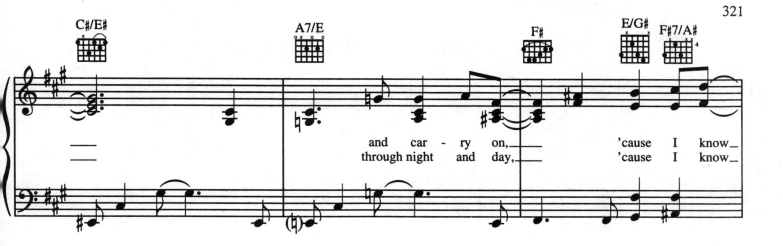

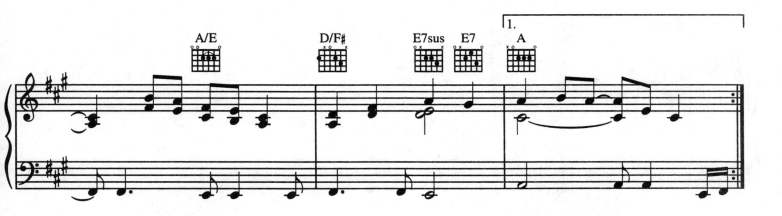

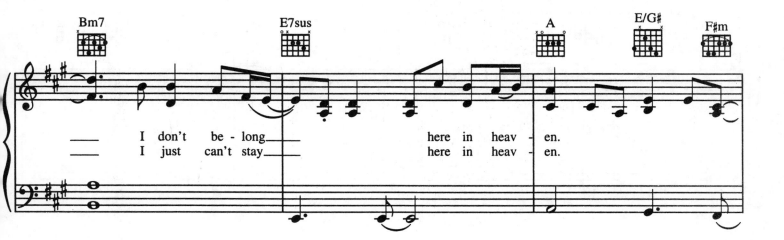

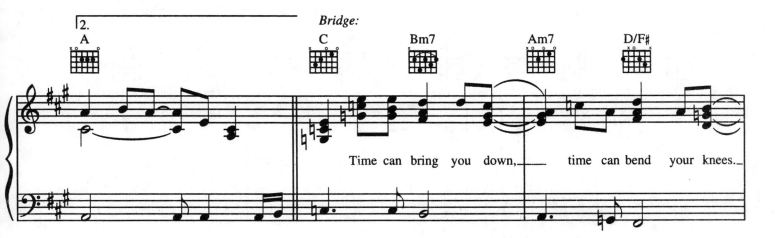

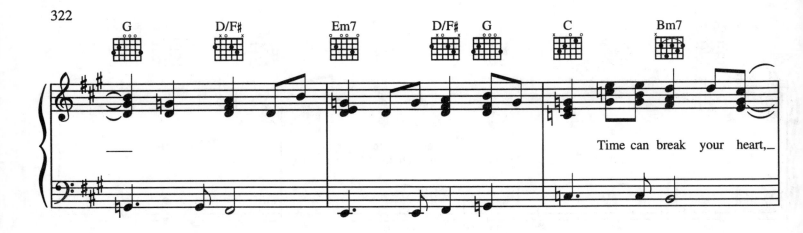

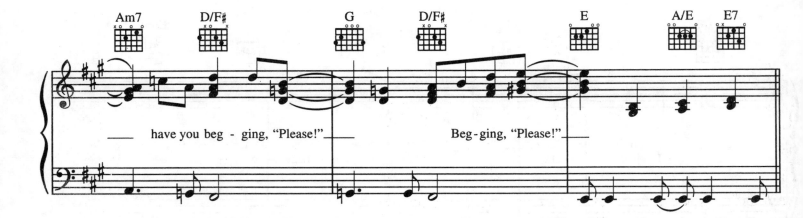

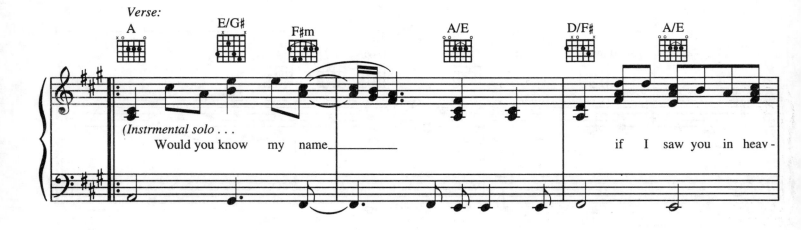

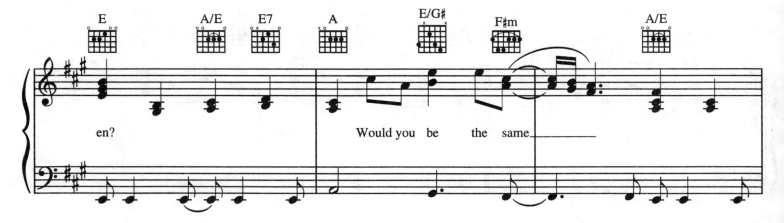

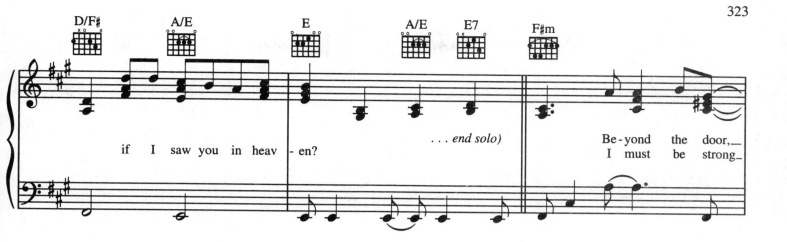

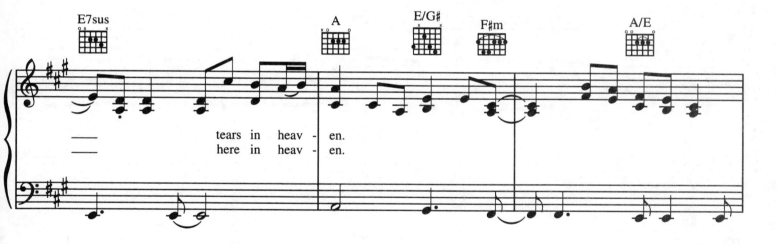

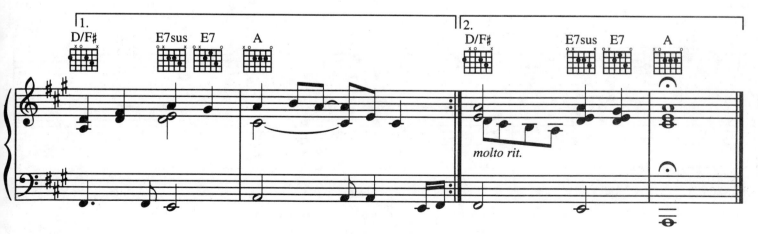

TELL HIM

Words and Music by
LINDA THOMPSON, DAVID FOSTER
and WALTER AFANASIEFF

Tell Him - 6 - 1

hand. But what you must un - der - stand, you can't let the

chance to love him pass you by._____

Chorus:

Both:

Tell_____ him, tell him_____ that the sun and moon rise

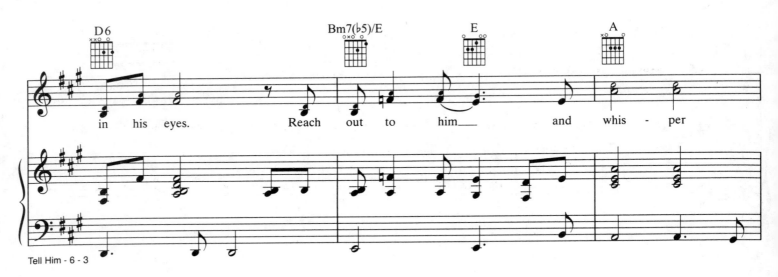

in his eyes. Reach out to him____ and whis - per

Tell Him - 6 - 3

grows._____ Feed the fire with all the pas - sion you can show._ To - night,_

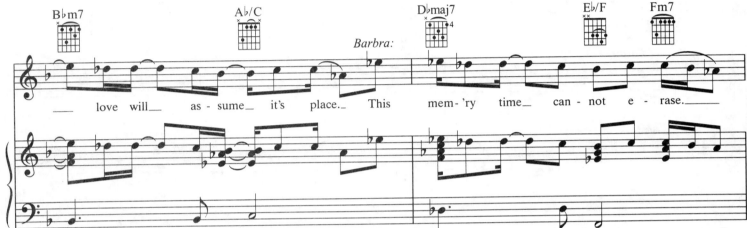

_ love will_ as - sume_ it's place._ This mem - 'ry time_ can - not e - rase._

Your faith will lead love where it has to_ go._

_ Tell_ him, tell him_ that the sun and moon rise in his eyes. Reach

Verse 2:
(Barbra:)
Touch him with the gentleness you feel inside. (C: I feel it.)
Your love can't be denied.
The truth will set you free.
You'll have what's meant to be.
All in time, you'll see.
(Celine:)
I love him, (B: Then show him.)
Of that much I can be sure. (B: Hold him close to you.)
I don't think I could endure
If I let him walk away
When I have so much to say.
(To Chorus:)

From the Twentieth Century Fox Motion Picture

THAT THING YOU DO!

Words and Music by
ADAM SCHLESINGER

1. You_____ do-in' that thing you do._____ And I'm
2. I_____ know all the games you play._____ And I'm
3. *(Guitar solo ad lib....*

Break-in' my heart in - to a mil - lion piec - es
gon - na find a way to let__ you know__ that

That Thing You Do! - 4 - 1

THINK TWICE

Words and Music by
ANDY HILL and PETE SINFIELD

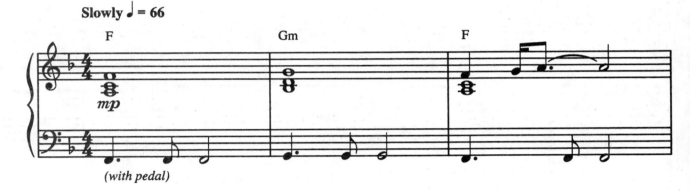

Verse:
1. Don't think I can't feel that there's some-thing wrong.

You've been the sweet-est part of__ my life__ for so____ long. I look in your eyes there's a

dis - tant light,_____ and you and I know_____ there'll be a storm to - night.__

Think Twice - 3 - 1

Gm — This is get-ting ser - i - ous.

C — Gm7 — cresc. — Are you think-ing 'bout

§ § Chorus:

C — you or us? 1.-3.,5. Don't say what you're a - bout to say. Look back

F — Bb — C

mf

F — be-fore you leave my life.

Am — Bb — C — Be sure be-fore you close that door,

F — Bb

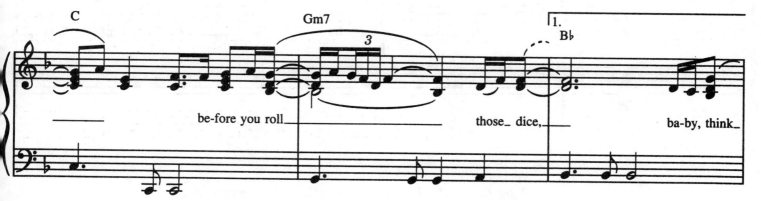

C — be-fore you roll those dice, baby, think

Gm7 — 3

1.
Bb

F — twice.

Gm — D.S. §

2.
Bb — 2. Ba-by, think ba-by, think

To next strain

3.4. etc. — Repeat ad lib. and fade

Bb — 4. Don't do
5. Don't say

Think Twice - 3 - 2

Verse 2:
Baby, think twice for the sake of our love, for the memory,
For the fire and the faith that was you and me.
Baby, I know it ain't easy when your soul cries out for higher ground,
'Cos when you're halfway up, you're always halfway down.
But baby, this is serious.
Are you thinking 'bout you or us?
(To Chorus:)

Chorus 4:
Don't do what you're about to do.
My everything depends on you,
And whatever it takes, I'll sacrifice.
Before you roll those dice,
Baby, think twice.

2 BECOME 1

Words and Music by
SPICE GIRLS, MATTHEW ROWEBOTTOM
and RICHARD STANNARD

2 Become 1 - 5 - 1

be for real—don't be— a stran-ger. We can a-chieve—it, we can a-chieve— it.—

— Come a lit-tle bit clo-ser ba-by,— get it on, get it on,— 'cause to-night—

— is the night— when two be-come one.— I

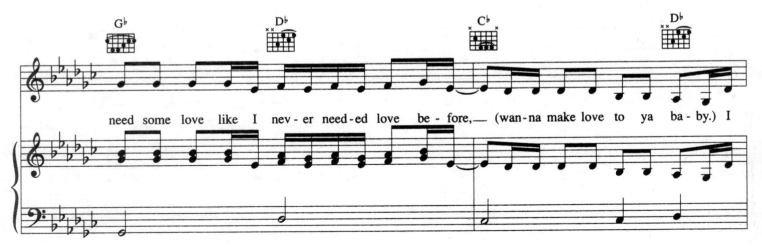

need some love like I nev-er need-ed love be-fore,— (wan-na make love to ya ba-by.) I

339

had a lit-tle love now I'm back for more, (wan-na make love to ya ba-by.)

Set your spi-rit free,— it's the on-ly way— to be.—

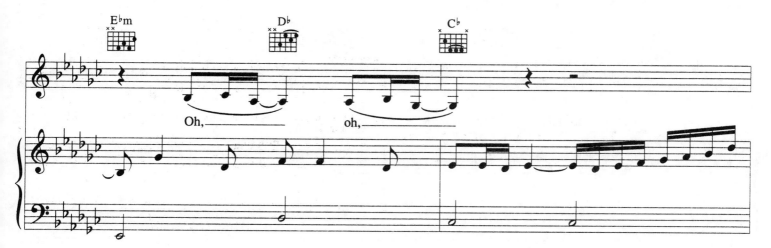

Oh,——— oh,———

2 Become 1 - 5 - 3

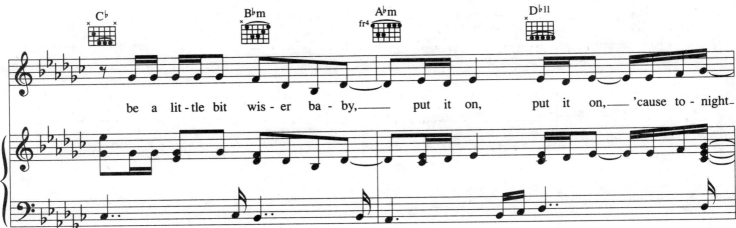

need some love like I nev-er need-ed love be-fore,— (wan-na make love to ya ba-by.) I

had a lit-tle love, now I'm back for more, (wan-na make love to ya ba-by.)

Repeat to fade

Set your spi-rit free,— it's the on-ly way to be.— It's the

Verse 2:

Silly games that you were playing, empty words we both were saying,
Let's work it out boy, let's work it out boy.
Any deal that we endeavour, boys and girls feel good together,
Take it or leave it, take it or leave it.
Are you as good as I remember baby, get it on, get it on,
'Cause tonight is the night when two become one.

I need some love like I never needed love before, (wanna make love to ya baby.)
I had a little love, now I'm back for more, (wanna make love to ya baby.)
Set your spirit free, it's the only way to be.

TOO LATE, TOO SOON

Words and Music by
JON SECADA, JAMES HARRIS III
and TERRY LEWIS

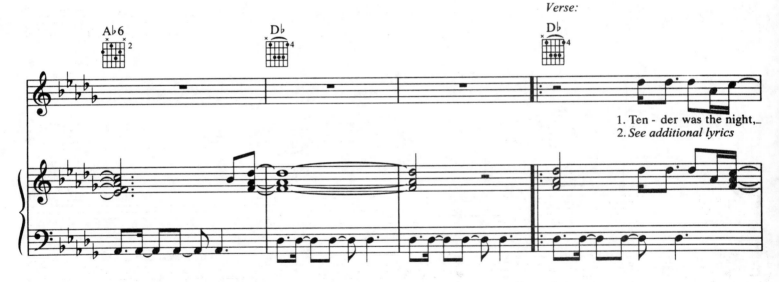

Too Late, Too Soon - 4 - 1

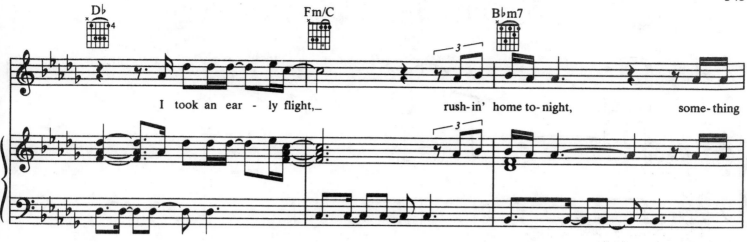

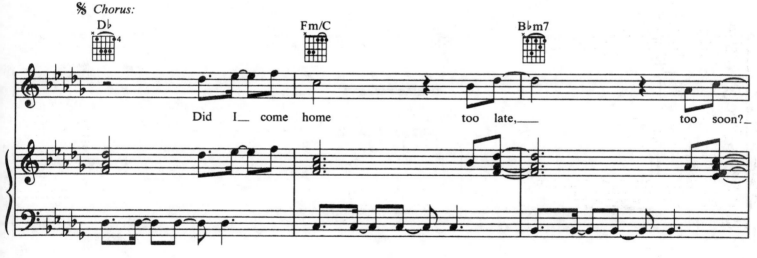

Too Late, Too Soon - 4 - 2

344

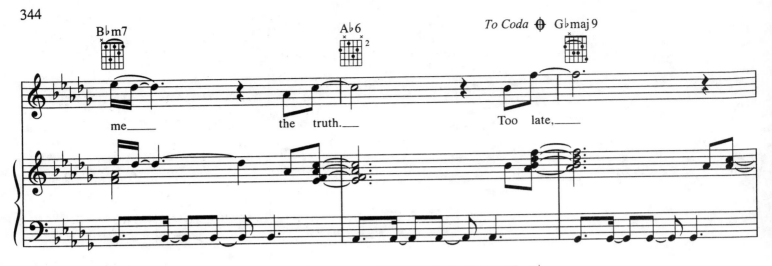

me___ the truth.___ Too late,___

too soon.___ too soon,___ ba - by,___ yeah..

What was I sup-posed to do? Oh.___

You had to see it for your-self,___

Verse 2:
I wish I would have known,
I wouldn't have left you all alone.
Temptation led you wrong.
Tell me how long this has been goin' on?
'Cause I thought our love was strong,
But I guess I must be dreamin'.
(To Chorus:)

Too Late, Too Soon - 4 - 4

UN-BREAK MY HEART

Words and Music by
DIANE WARREN

Repeat ad lib. and fade

THE WAY SHE LOVES ME

Music and Lyrics by
RICHARD MARX

The Way She Loves Me - 3 - 1

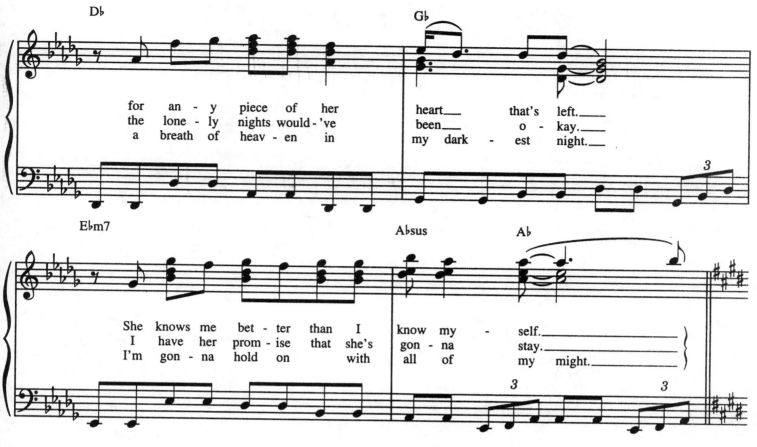

for an - y piece of her heart___ that's left.___
the lone - ly nights would - 've been___ o - kay.
a breath of heav - en in my dark - est night.___

She knows me bet - ter than I know my - self.___
I have her prom - ise that she's gon - na stay.___
I'm gon - na hold on with all of my might.___

Chorus:

Let me tell you 'bout the way she loves_ me. Ooh,___ I want the world to know.___

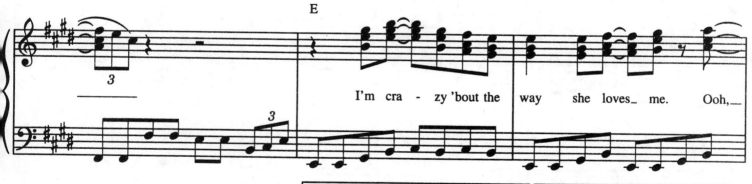

I'm cra - zy 'bout the way she loves_ me. Ooh,___

___ I'm proud to let it show.___

| 1. 2. | *D.S.* 𝄋 | 3. | *Repeat ad lib. and fade* |

The Way She Loves Me - 3 - 3

UNTIL I FIND YOU AGAIN

Music and Lyrics by
RICHARD MARX

Moderately slow ♩ = 76

Verse:

1. Late - ly I've been try - ing to fill up my days since you're gone.
2. Well, the arms of hope sur - round me. Will time be a fair weath - er friend?

The speed of love is blind - ing and I
Should I call out to an - gels or just

did - n't know how to hold on. My mind won't clear, I'm out
drink my - self sob - er a - gain? I can't hide this truth, I still burn

Until I Find You Again - 4 - 1

F   Dm7   Gsus   G

— of tears,__ my heart's__ got no room__ left in - side.___ }
— for you.__ Your mem - 'ry just won't__ let me go.____

% *Chorus:*

C   F/C   G/C   G7(♭9)/C

1.2. How man - y dreams__ will end?____ How long can I____ pre - tend?__
— 3. *(Inst. solo ad lib....*

C   Am   Dm7   *To Coda* ⊕

— How man - y times__ will love___ pass me by__ un -

C/G   G   **1.** F   C   **2.** C

til I find you_____ a - gain?__

VALENTINE

Composed by
JIM BRICKMAN and JACK KUGELL

Valentine - 6 - 1

362

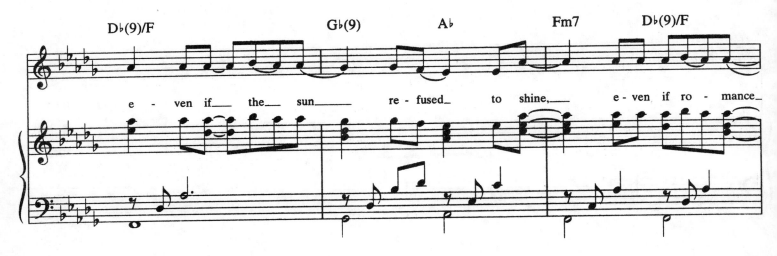

Valentine - 6 - 5

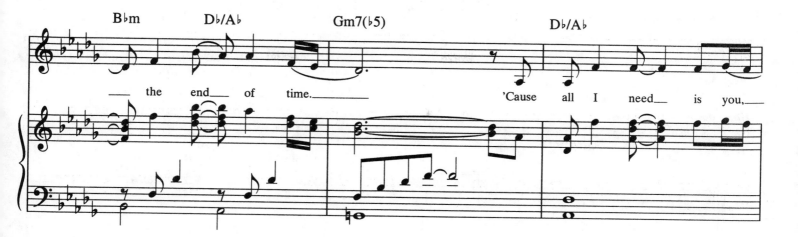

Valentine - 6 - 6

WALKIN' ON THE SUN

Words and Music by
STEVE HARWELL, GREGORY CAMP,
PAUL DeLISLE and KEVIN COLEMAN

Walkin' on the Sun - 6 - 1

Verse 2:
Twenty-five years ago they spoke out
And they broke out of recession and oppression.
And together they toked and they folked out with guitars
Around a bonfire, just singin' and clappin'; man, what the hell happened?
Yeah, some were spellbound, some were hell bound,
Some, they fell down and some got back up and fought back against the meltdown.
And their kids were hippie chicks, all hypocrites
Because their fashion is smashin' the true meaning of it.
(To Chorus:)

WHEN I DIE

Words and Music by
DIANE WARREN, FRANK FARIAN, DIETMAR KAWOHL
and PETER BISCHOF-FALLENSTEIN

need you,   yes, I____ do.

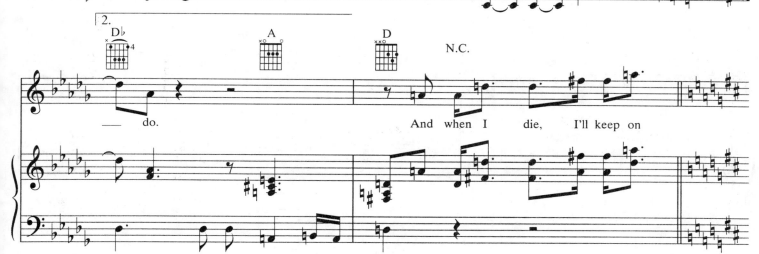

____ do.   And when I   die,   I'll keep on

Chorus:

liv - ing.   You'll al - ways have   my love___

WHO WILL SAVE YOUR SOUL

Words and Music by
JEWEL KILCHER

Moderate shuffle feel ♩ = 112

Verse:

1. Peo - ple liv - in' their lives for you__ on T__ V,__ they say they're bet - ter than you__ and

you a - gree.__ She says hold__ my calls from be - hind those cold,__ brick walls. She says

Who Will Save Your Soul - 7 - 1

af - ter all those lies___ that you told,___ boy?

Who will save_____ your soul if you won't

save your own?___ La da da da__ di da da la da da__ ya__ die.__

___

2. We try to hus - tle them, try to bus -
3. Some are walk - ing, some are talk -

Who Will Save Your Soul - 7 - 3

378

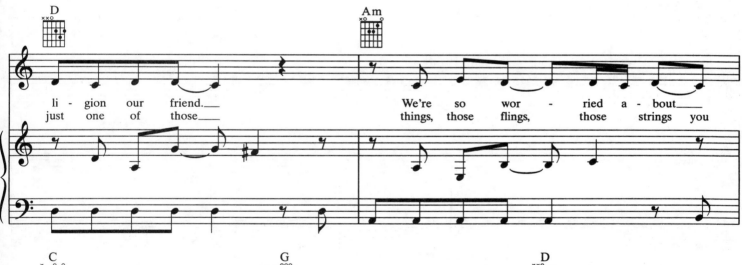

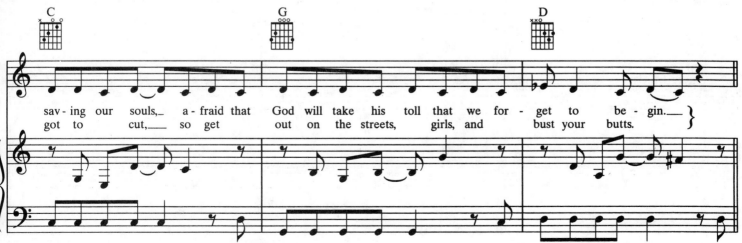

Chorus:

who__ will save_____ your soul,___ when it comes__

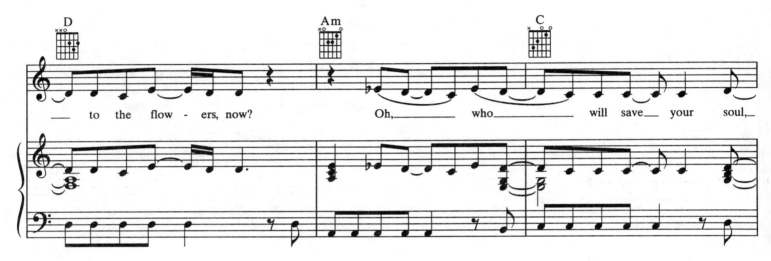

__ to the flow - ers, now? Oh,_____ who_____ will save__ your soul,__

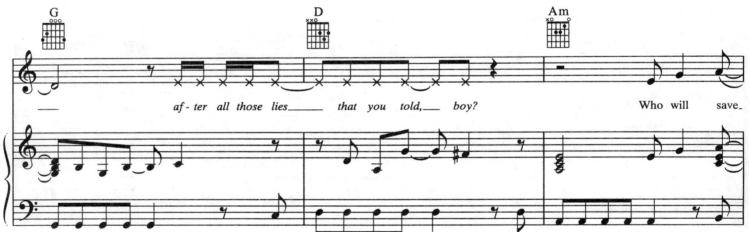

__ af - ter all those lies_____ that you told,___ boy? Who will save__

_____ your soul if you won't save your own?_____

La da da da___ di da da la da da___ ya___ die.___

Repeat ad lib. and fade

Di da da, di da da, da die ya___ ba da.

WHERE'S THE LOVE

Words and Music by
ISAAC HANSON, TAYLOR HANSON,
ZACHARY HANSON, MARK HUDSON
and STEVEN SALOVER

Verse:

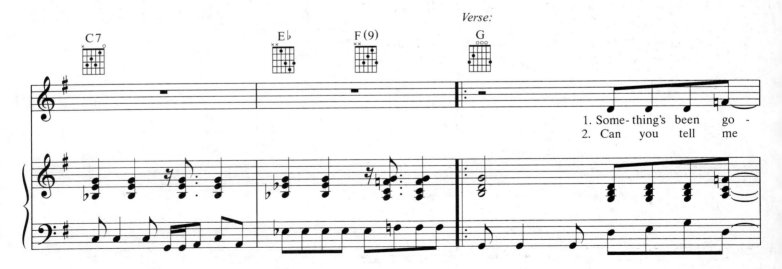

1. Some-thing's been go -
2. Can you tell me

Where's the Love - 6 - 1

'round and 'round_ and 'round.____

Dark clouds all a - round,_ light - ning, rain pour-ing down._

We're wait- ing for the bright light to break through. Face down on the ground,_

pick us up_ at the lost and found. We've got to change our point of view_ if we want the sky blue._

Where's the Love - 6 - 4

YOU ARE NOT ALONE

Written and Composed by
R. KELLY

You Are Not Alone - 7 - 1

G#m7 / C#m7

did you have_ to go
but first I need_ your hand,
and leave my world_ so
so for - ev - er can be -

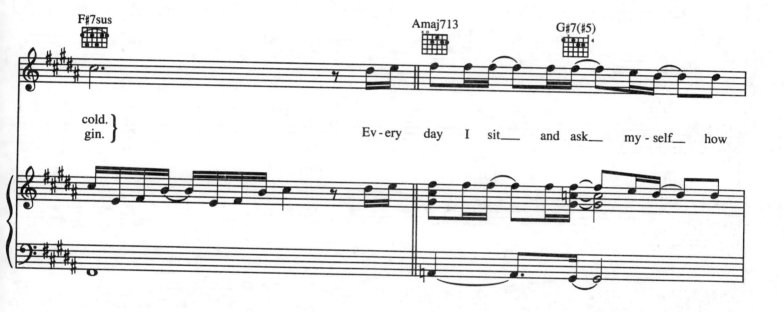

F#7sus / Amaj713 / G#7(#5)

cold.
gin.

Ev - ery day I sit_ and ask_ my - self_ how

E / C#m7

did love slip_ a - way._

Some - thing whis - pers in my ear_ and says:_

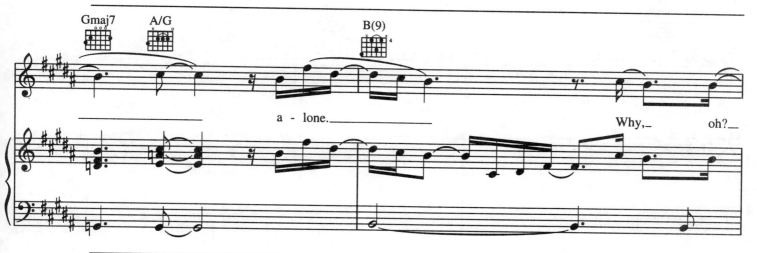

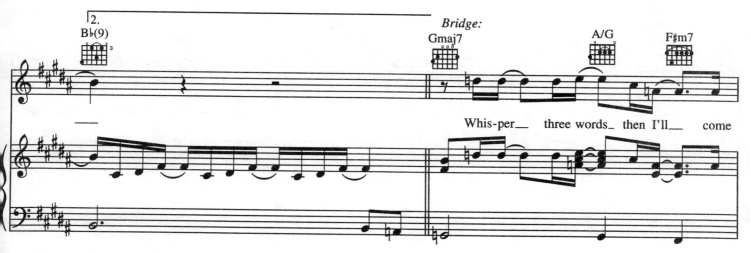

YOU'RE MAKIN' ME HIGH

Words and Music by
BRYCE WILSON and BABYFACE

You're Makin' Me High - 5 - 1

398

399

You're Makin' Me High - 5 - 5

YOU'LL SEE

Words and Music by
MADONNA CICCONE and
DAVID FOSTER

You'll See - 4 - 1

You think I have noth - ing_____ with - out___ you by___
You think af - ter all you've done,___ I'll nev - er find my way___
I have truth on my side,___ you on - ly have

___ my side.___ You'll see,___ some - how,___ some way.___
___ back home.___ You'll see,___ some - how,___ some - day.___
___ de - ceit. You'll see,___ some - how,___ some - day.___

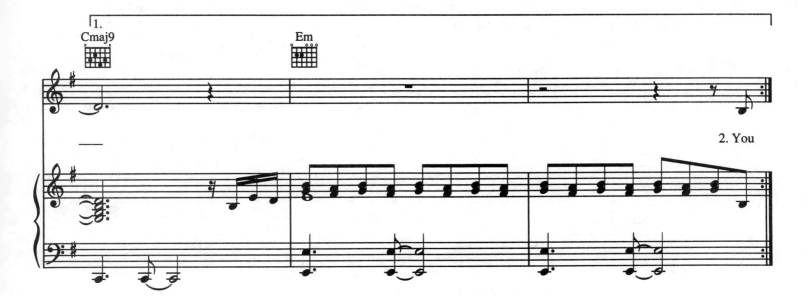

2. You

take it from me,___   you'll see.___

To Coda ⊕   *D.S.* 𝄋 *al Coda*

3. You

⊕ *Coda*

You'll see.___   You'll see,__

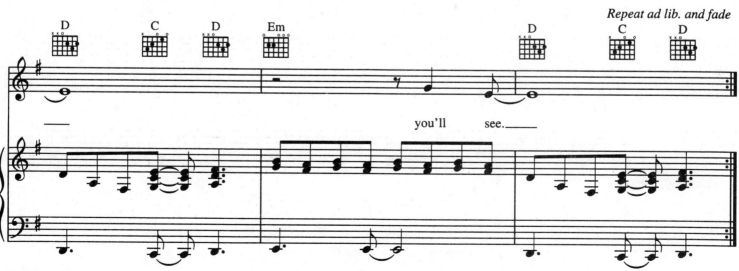

Repeat ad lib. and fade

you'll see.___

You'll See - 4 - 4

YOU'RE NOT ALONE

Words and Music by
TIM KELLETT and ROBIN TAYLOR-FIRTH

*1st time omit left hand.

You're Not Alone - 5 - 1

I'll wait till the end___ of time___ for you.___

O - pen your mind.___ Sure - ly, there's time___

to be___ with me.___

|1.

|2.

*Begin left hand.

Verse 2:
It is the distance that makes life a little hard.
Two minds that once were close, now so many miles apart.
I will not falter, though I'll hold on till you're home,
Safely back where you belong, and see how our love has grown.
(To Chorus:)

You're Not Alone - 5 - 5

YOU WERE MEANT FOR ME

Words and Music by
JEWEL KILCHER and STEVE POLTZ

You Were Meant for Me - 5 - 1

Verse 2:
I called my mama, she was out for a walk.
Consoled a cup of coffee, but it didn't wanna talk.
So I picked up a paper, it was more bad news,
More hearts being broken or people being used.
Put on my coat in the pouring rain.
I saw a movie, it just wasn't the same,
'Cause it was happy and I was sad,
And it made me miss you, oh, so bad.
(To Chorus:)

Verse 3:
I brush my teeth and put the cap back on,
I know you hate it when I leave the light on.
I pick a book up and then I turn the sheets down,
And then I take a breath and a good look around.
Put on my pj's and hop into bed.
I'm half alive but I feel mostly dead.
I try and tell myself it'll be all right,
I just shouldn't think anymore tonight.
(To Chorus:)

COUNTDOWN SERIES

60s COUNTDOWN
Pop, Rock & Soul Decade

Piano/Vocal/Chords
___ **(F3031SMX)**

HEY, MAN! Check this out! A sensational collection of 76 gre
tunes from the Psychedelic Sixties. Includes: When Will I Be L
(The Everly Brothers 1960) ● Do You Love Me (The Contours 1
● Oh, Pretty Woman (Roy Orbison 1964) ● The Tracks of My T
(Miracles 1965) ● A Place in the Sun (Stevie Wonder 196
Aquarius/Let the Sunshine In (5th Dimension 1969).

70's COUNTDOWN
A DECADE OF CLASSIC HITS!

Piano/Vocal/Chords
___ **(F3045SMX)**

Bring back memories with 65 classic hits like: The Tears of a C
(Miracles 1970) ● American Pie (Don McLean 1972) ● My
Adored You (Frankie Valli 1975) ● Nobody Does It Better (C
Simon 1977) ● Three Times a Lady (Commodores 1978) ● Old
Rock & Roll (Bob Seger 1979).

80's COUNTDOWN
A Decade of POP HITS!

Piano/Vocal/Chords
___ **(F3000SMX) Perfect-bound**
___ **(F3000SMS) Spiral-bound**
Big Note Piano
___ **(F3000P3X)**
Easy Piano
___ **(F3000P2X)**

An extravaganza of exciting pop music. 103 titles including: A
All (Love Theme from *Chances Are)* (Cher and Peter Cetera 198
Anything for You (Gloria Estefan and Miami Sound Machine 1
● Babe (Styx 1980) ● Back in the High Life Again (Steve Winw
1987) ● Cold-Hearted (Paula Abdul 1989) ● Glory of Love (The
from *The Karate Kid Part II)* (Peter Cetera 1986) ● The Lady in
(Chris DeBurgh 1987) ● Money for Nothing (Dire Straits 1986)

80's COUNTDOWN
A Decade of COUNTRY HITS!

Piano/Vocal/Chords
___ **(F3001SMX)**

We're talkin' **COUNTRY MUSIC** now! A host of country stars and
of their biggest hits are in this collection including: All My Ro
Friends Are Coming Over Tonight (Hank Williams, Jr. 1985) ● El
(The Oak Ridge Boys 1981) ● Forever and Ever, Amen (Ra
Travis 1987) ● Nine to Five (Dolly Parton 1981) ● The Vows
Unbroken (Always True to You) (Kenny Rogers 1989) ● Wh
Going on in Your World (George Strait 1989) ● You and I (Ec
Rabbitt and Crystal Gayle 1982) ● Young Love (The Judds 198

howstoppers

100 or more titles in each volume of this Best-Selling Series!

The Book of *Golden* Series

THE BOOK OF GOLDEN ALL-TIME FAVORITES
(F2939SMX) Piano/Vocal/Chords

THE BOOK OF GOLDEN BIG BAND FAVORITES
(F3172SMX) Piano/Vocal/Chords

THE BOOK OF GOLDEN BROADWAY
(F2986SMX) Piano/Vocal/Chords

THE NEW BOOK OF GOLDEN CHRISTMAS
(F2478SMB) Piano/Vocal/Chords
(F2478EOX) Easy Organ
(F2478COX) Chord Organ

THE BOOK OF GOLDEN COUNTRY MUSIC
(F2926SMA) Piano/Vocal/Chords

THE BOOK OF GOLDEN HAWAIIAN SONGS
(F3113SMX) Piano/Vocal/Chords

THE BOOK OF GOLDEN IRISH SONGS
(F3212SMX) Piano/Vocal/Chords

THE BOOK OF GOLDEN ITALIAN SONGS
(F2907SMX) Piano/Vocal/Chords

THE BOOK OF GOLDEN JAZZ
(F3012SMX) Piano/Vocal/Chords

THE NEW BOOK OF GOLDEN LATIN SONGS
(F3049SMX) Piano/Vocal/Chords

THE NEW BOOK OF GOLDEN LOVE SONGS
(F2415SOX) Organ

THE BOOK OF GOLDEN MOTOWN SONGS
(F3144SMX) Piano/Vocal/Chords

THE NEW BOOK OF GOLDEN MOVIE THEMES, Volume 1
(F2810SMX) Piano/Vocal/Chords

THE NEW BOOK OF GOLDEN MOVIE THEMES, Volume 2
(F2811SMX) Piano/Vocal/Chords

THE BOOK OF GOLDEN POPULAR FAVORITES
(F2233SMX) Piano/Vocal/Chords

THE BOOK OF GOLDEN POPULAR PIANO SOLOS
(F3193P9X) Intermediate/
Advanced Piano

THE BOOK OF GOLDEN ROCK 'N' ROLL
(F2830SMB) Piano/Vocal/Chords

THE NEW BOOK OF GOLDEN WEDDING SONGS
(F2265SMA) Piano/Vocal/Chords